Praise for *Be Bold*

"Rachel Billups is a powerful communicator who has the vision and courage to move where the Spirit is moving into God's next. A great read for all leaders!"

Mike Slaughter
Pastor Emeritus, Ginghamsburg Church,
Founder and Chief Strategist, Passionate Churches, LLC

"'Crossover Credentials' is a term I've used to describe leaders who use their seemingly disparate gifts toward incredible purposes. Rachel Billups is such a leader. Her "thin slice of life" roots, her Enneagram #8, and her passionate call to ministry render her the best possible person to write this book with authenticity and candor. Her stories will engage you and her truth will challenge you to reach down and find your own amazing fierce."

Kim Miller
Author of *Redesigning Churches* and *Redesigning Worship*

"*Be Bold* is a masterful weaving together of sacred scripture and personal story. Rachel humbly shows us the highlight reel of her life as well as vulnerably shows us the blooper reel too. She wonderfully helps Christ followers hear the whisper of the God who makes the mundane and mess of our lives into a masterpiece. This book will help you become fully alive in Christ living into the best you that you can become."

Jorge Acevedo
Lead Pastor, Grace Church

"Being bold can mean many different things. For Rachel Billups, her boldness is rooted in spiritual honesty, biblical wisdom, and a prophetic witness that lovingly convicts us into communion with Christ. *Be Bold: Finding Your Fierce* invites us to recognize how powerful the spiritual discipline of affirmation is in transforming our past into fuel for our Christian journey."

Matt Rawle
Author of *The Redemption of Scrooge*,
Lead Pastor, Asbury United Methodist Church,
Bossier City, Louisiana

"For years, Rachel Billups has modeled a bold and courageous life, lived for Christ. Thankfully, she has now put into words how we too can face the future unafraid. You may have never seen yourself as fierce, but after reading this book you will!"

Jacob Armstrong
Pastor, Providence Church, Mt. Juliet, Tennessee,
Author of *The New Adapters, Renovate, A New Playlist*,
and *God's Messy Family*

"Rachel Billups is one of the most talented younger clergy throughout the country. Through her insightful work, *Be Bold: Finding Your Fierce*, she is real, raw, and confessional about her journey in finding her fierce and God-given leadership mantle. By reading her work, you can't help but feel challenged to grow in the next step of your leadership journey."

Rev. Dr. Rosario "Roz" Picardo
Dean of The Chapel and Director of The Pohly Center
for Supervision and Leadership Formation, United
Theological Seminary, Co-Pastor of Mosaic Church

"Rachel Billups lives life full out as a fierce, focused, no limits, on-fire pastor, leader, and Jesus follower—and yes, that's also a pretty good description of *Be Bold*. Readers will enjoy the gift of fierce."

Karen Perry Smith
Senior Executive Director of Leadership Development
& Missional Strategy, Ginghamsburg Church

BE
BOLD

Finding Your Fierce

Rachel Billups

ABINGDON PRESS
NASHVILLE

BE BOLD
FINDING YOUR FIERCE

Copyright © 2019 Abingdon Press

Library of Congress Cataloging-in-Publication data has been requested.

978-1-5018-7920-3

19 20 21 22 23 24 25 26 27 28—10 9 8 7 6 5 4 3 2 1
MANUFACTURED IN THE UNITED STATES OF AMERICA

CONTENTS

INTRODUCTION

I'm a lemonade master. You might think my life's lemons are better than yours. They may seem brighter with fewer rotten spots, but yeah, they are lemons nonetheless. Just because there are sour moments in life, however, doesn't mean that God's going to throw out the whole batch of lemonade. My life has not always been easy, but I've learned, through the sour spots, to overcome obstacles, name fears, and use failure to fuel what I call my "fierce"—a holy boldness that has emerged from pain, frustration, silence, and breakthrough.

Be Bold: Finding Your Fierce is an invitation to journey with me. Together, we will peel back the layers of life. We will name the struggle and the suffering (self-inflicted and otherwise), and we'll recognize how it all—the good, the bad, and the in-between—can fuel our fierce.

Be Bold: Finding Your Fierce is part life story and part Bible narrative, capped off with a conversation with you about how I discovered fierce in a way that has changed not only my life but also the lives of people around me. It is the story of how fierce can change your life too! You do not have to live your whole life wishing that you could overcome the obstacles to being fully alive and living into your fierce. With the likes of David, Deborah, Moses, Esther, and Jesus, we will discover the ups and downs that lead people to stop playing life small and recognize God's purpose and potential in their lives. I want you to finish this book empowered to embrace your past as fuel for your fierce but not to be bound by the limitation prophecies—the words of others or those inner thoughts that tell us we can't be who we are—that sometimes characterize your present.

This journey is your opportunity to tell yourself the truth about yourself. Be sure to be kind! Give yourself a little grace along the way. You have too many critics already and certainly do not need to become your own. My hope is that you will close this book having laughed, cried, and been inspired to live differently. I want you to strategize, to plan, to dream a dream of fierce possibilities for your future. Why do I have this dream for you? Because it is my dream for my life too!

Chapters 1 and 2 challenge us to wrestle with the limitation prophecies that people speak over us. Those negative words have the potential to cap our fierce, and you may discover that these limitation prophecies are your source of fear. Chapters 3 and 4 give us an opportunity to confess that we speak limiting words over one another as well, but we also recognize just how powerful our fierce can be when we fight for the right stuff. I wrote chapter 5 on my wedding anniversary because I wanted to give a picture of what fierce can do in a real-life marriage—the good and the bad. And then comes the hard stuff, chapters 6, 7, and 8—those moments in my life where I discovered fierce through silence, pressure, and pain. Chapter 9 is a reminder that we are bold because others have shaped our boldness. Finally, in chapter 10, I show how our fierce identity becomes the fuel to be fully alive.

I'm on the hunt for a life fully lived. I can't get there without looking back, being present, and propelling forward all at the same time. I have to keep going, even when I don't want to, even when I would rather quit, even when everyone around me gives me permission to hang it up. Myself, my true child-of-God self, pushes me from within to say, "I cannot quit, not now! I cannot stop believing, dreaming, and moving forward! There is more to life! There is fierce! *Let's be bold!*"

LIMITATION PROPHECIES

So he asked Jesse, "Are these all the sons you have?" "There is still the youngest," Jesse answered. "He is tending the sheep." Samuel said, "Send for him; we will not sit down until he arrives."

1 Samuel 16:11

I am a sucker for a great underdog story. I love to watch people overcome the odds to achieve the kinds of things that most of us only dream about. David had some advantages, though, when it came to defeating and killing the Philistine giant Goliath. He certainly had a limitation prophecy spoken over him by his family. He was the runt, the youngest one, and the tender of the sheep. Although this was an important job in the family circle, his older brothers were out doing much more important things for the family. They served in the military; they defended God's people against enemy armies. While the older brothers were out saving the world, the youngest was stuck at home seemingly serving his entire family. Although David's family situation was ripe for resentment, it seemed that neither David nor his brothers were particularly bothered by the roles they played. Perhaps it's because the culture had clear expectations for sons within their designated birth orders. But David perceived his lot in life as a training ground for what could happen in his future. Limitation prophecies were not the end of David's story and they are not the end of ours either.

Words are powerful. They shape the way we see God and others, and they certainly shape the way we see ourselves. Although we may attempt to downplay the effect of words with expressions such as, "Sticks and stones may break my bones, but words will never hurt me," the reality is that words can devastate a human being from the inside out. In the Gospel of Matthew, Jesus had something to say about the power of our words: "What goes into someone's mouth does not defile them, but what comes out of their mouth, that is what defiles them" (Matthew 15:11). Life-giving words are freedom, but even when we think the world should be a very different place, a limitation prophecy can bind us to the social reality we live in—it can box us in.

> Words are powerful. They shape the way we see God and others, and they certainly shape the way we see ourselves.

Boxed In

When I was five years old, I remember standing in my bedroom, gathering my clothes. Flannel shirt, check. Long jeans, check. Farm boots, check—everything I thought I would need to bale hay that day. Even though we baled hay in pretty hot temperatures, it was critical to cover all parts of the body that you didn't want scratched. I slipped into my blue jeans, pulled on a white undershirt, and was getting ready to ask my mom to braid my hair when my older brother Jason said to me, "What do you think you are doing?"

"I'm getting ready, same as you!" I piped back.

My brother was nearly three years older than I was, but because I had grown faster than he had, we were almost the same height.

"Will Dad let you bale hay?" he asked.

"*Let me?*" The thought had never crossed my mind that Dad would not let me bale hay. There was hay to bale and hands to help, and whenever there was work to do on the farm, nearly everyone was needed to chip in. "Of course Dad will let me," I said.

When Dad came into the house, he said, "Jason, let's go!"

"Dad!" I yelled, "I am almost ready, too!"

I came out of my room dressed and ready to go. All I needed were my farm boots. "Rach," Dad said, "what do you think you are doing? You can't bale hay."

"But, Dad," I protested, "I am just as big as Jason. I can help!"

"Rachel, I don't have time to keep an eye on you, and besides we've got plenty of help today." Dad rattled off the names of all the men and boys in the neighborhood whom he had enlisted to help bale that day. I'm sure I threw a fit and attempted to manipulate my way into baling. Finally, my dad, in exasperation, said, "No! Rachel, baling hay is no place for a young girl like yourself."

Those words hit me like a ton of bricks. I knew, even at five years old, that they were meant to keep me in my place.

At the time, I wasn't aware of the beer-drinking, tobacco-chewing, lewd-joking culture that the neighborhood men fully embraced when baling hay. I just knew that my help wasn't wanted because I wasn't a boy. Translation: Little girls don't bale hay. A fierce anger grew within in me. I tried to reason with my mom, but she wouldn't hear it. She had other plans for me. I am sure I was assigned to pick green beans or to pick bugs off the potato plants. Whatever it was, my family was telling me that certain genders do certain work. Even though I didn't believe what they were saying, I began to step into a limitation prophecy that I would struggle with my whole life. Our culture has a lid for your life—your gender.

Have you ever had a limitation prophecy spoken over you? Words that limited your view of yourself and the world you find yourself in? Such messages are not limited to gender, race, or ethnicity. Perhaps it's where you grew up, the hand you were dealt in life, a circumstance that was beyond your control—but whatever your lot in life, with just some simple words, someone told you to stay put and remain in your place. You felt the box closing in on you!

These limiting words in our lives are not always direct. Sometimes they are passed from generation to generation.

The Family Way

I come from a long line of women who have had to battle for their fierce. Both of my grandmothers were bold and are still. My paternal grandmother Ruby could "curse the flowers off of wall paper." She served as one of the first female township trustees for the state of Ohio, and when my grandpa Paul died of a massive heart attack, she found out the day after the funeral that she had non-Hodgkin's lymphoma. She battled cancer for thirteen more years. Ruby was no stranger to fierce. But neither was my maternal grandmother, Marcella Marie Goodman.

One Sunday afternoon, I was sitting in my Grandma Marie's kitchen. It was after church, and I was hanging out with my serious boyfriend at the time. My grandma enjoyed talking about church and Jesus. So when we started talking about my plans after high school, she seemed a little frustrated and confused.

She asked with serious reservation in her voice, "Are you all planning on getting married?"

It's an awkward question to have to address when your boyfriend is in the room. At the same time, it didn't seem odd to me that my grandmother would ask that question. There was an expectation in the Hocking Hills where I grew up that if you were serious with someone, you should consider getting married. Folks got married young; it's what they did. So while I was quite unsure of my future with this boyfriend, I piped back, "Well, yes, Grandma, someday we hope to be married to each other."

But my answer seemed to disturb my grandmother.

"Why would you do that?" she demanded. At this point, I was a little embarrassed for my boyfriend, Jon. I couldn't tell whether she was attempting to drop a not-so-subtle hit about her disapproval of Jon or had legitimate questions about my getting married.

"Well, Grandma, don't you want me to get married someday?" I jokingly replied.

"Are you going to college?" she asked.

"Why yes," I said.

"Then why go to college if you are going to just get married? Why waste all of that money?"

I can't remember what I said next. I pray that it wasn't too harsh or rude or just plain mean. In that moment I realized my grandma had lived with an assumption: people who go to college don't get married and don't have families. And people who don't go to college do have families. It was that black and white for my grandmother. If I was planning on having a family, I shouldn't go to college.

I didn't stay long. I had a habit of telling people exactly what I thought, and I knew myself well enough to know that if I wanted to remain in my grandmother's good graces, I didn't need to speak what was on my mind. But I realized in that moment that Grandma Marie was just speaking the same limitation prophecy over me that had been spoken over her: "Stay in your lane: get married, have children, and enjoy it. This is your lot in life." This was Marie's truth.

I can't imagine all the limitation prophecies that must have been spoken over my Grandma Marie. She had grown up poor, one of eleven children who experienced the harsh realities of rural poverty: addiction, abuse, and limited access to resources, including education. My grandmother's life picture was extremely limited. The situation in her household was so painful that, by the time she was fifteen, she decided to run away and marry my grandfather, Edgel McNichols. Grandpa Edgel was thirty-three, and Marie became his literal child bride. She had given birth to five children by the time she was twenty-five.

Grandma Marie's life was hard and her marriage rocky, and my grandfather regularly spoke limits over her. "He became very possessive of me," my grandma once told me.

"Your Grandpa Edgel was afraid I would land in the arms of a younger man." Although my grandmother had a seed of faith, she didn't always attend church. She needed hope and healing. Soon, the rockiness of her marriage would lead to divorce and then marriage to my Grandpa Bud Goodman. Even though life got a little better for Grandma after remarriage, her life picture remained limited.

Growing up on the edges of Appalachia, I realized that most of what we humans know is what we've been taught to believe about ourselves. It takes fierce courage, both from outside and within, to give us a picture of the potential that lies beyond what we know.

God-Centered Hope

For all the crap that people say about organized religion, it was church that gave me a picture of my future possibilities. It wasn't because I understood what lay beyond the boundaries of Hocking County but rather because I knew that God looked at people with a different set of eyes. People like David.

Saul had been anointed king of Israel. And although the people of God seemed to be in alignment with their ruler, they certainly were not in alignment with God. Saul regularly decided to do his own thing, go his own way. After too many times of allowing his pride to lead him, God revoked Saul's royal anointing. This devastated Saul and left a gaping hole of political and spiritual leadership in the nation. So God decided to anoint a new king. But even Samuel, the messenger of God, struggled with God's decision.

> *The LORD said to Samuel, "How long will you mourn*
> *for Saul, since I have rejected him as king over Israel?*
> *Fill your horn with oil and be on your way; I am sending*
> *you to Jesse of Bethlehem. I have chosen one of his sons to*
> *be king." But Samuel said, "How can I go? If Saul hears*
> *about it, he will kill me." The LORD said, "Take a heifer*
> *with you and say, 'I have come to sacrifice to the LORD.'*
> *Invite Jesse to the sacrifice, and I will show you what to*
> *do. You are to anoint for me the one I indicate."*
>
> 1 Samuel 16:1-3

Samuel had a job to do: God had commissioned him to prepare the new ruler. Sometimes when we have to do something that we don't want to, our judgment and discernment can be altered. I can imagine that Samuel was in a little bit of an altered state when he arrived at Jesse's home. His grief for his king and his friend perhaps clouded his vision of what he perceived to be in front of him. Besides, Saul was seemingly the tallest man in Israel—a physical distinction that had become the standard for the king. Samuel asked Jesse to prepare his sons for worship.

"Samuel replied, 'Yes, in peace; I have come to sacrifice to the LORD. Consecrate yourselves and come to the sacrifice with me.' Then he consecrated Jesse and his sons and invited them to the sacrifice" (1 Samuel 16:5). Samuel attempted to see— that is, to discern—who was the next right king for Israel. But discernment is a funny thing. It's not just about what we see with our eyes or experience with our senses. Discernment requires a spiritual sense. It requires a nudge of the Holy Spirit to confirm what we perceive to be the next right move in our life and the lives of the people around us.

Discernment is not easy. It takes practice and requires intentional listening. I don't know about you, but listening is not a natural gift of mine—talking, speaking, giving advice, and inserting my opinion—that's natural; but listening for the voice of God in my life takes intentional spiritual concentration. And besides, lots of other noise is always crowding in—the limitation prophecies challenge my every thought: "I couldn't possibly do that. That big next step is beyond me. Stay in your lane, Rachel." Reading through the Bible now and as a young kid, the Scriptures gave me pictures of people who didn't allow the negative words spoken over their lives to determine their destiny.

Samuel had no intention of allowing his perceptions to shape his reality, but there he was, face to face with the lineup of Jesse's sons—young, strong men who knew how to fight for the right stuff. Samuel, distracted by his own grief and perception of what royalty looked like, began to ask God, "Is this the one?" first of Eliab, the tall one whose height, at the very least, caught Samuel's eye. "No, Samuel," God said. "Stop attempting to duplicate Saul. You are looking for some kind of outward indicator. You are looking for a natural gift, but I am not boxed in by natural limitations. Samuel, I can see what you cannot see. I can see into the heart," declared God. It was Saul's heart—his intentions—that had led Saul astray, so God was reminding Samuel that God can use anyone, no matter their physical limitations.

With each of Jesse's seven sons, Samuel asked, "Is this the one, God?" And each time, God said, "No!" In ancient Israel, birth order and birthright mattered! Yet Samuel walked by the so-called golden children—the favored ones, the ones destined for greatness—and then by the lesser ones before he even encountered David.

Not the Golden Child

You may have an assumption about me. Only "golden children" write books. They are the most successful, the most popular, and the most promoted by the family. Sometimes that's true, but I can assure you that I didn't start out as the "golden one." That title was my brother's. Jason is the oldest and the only son in our family of three. Looking back, I realize the unrealistic pressure that is sometimes placed on the oldest, and particularly on the oldest and only son in a family, who's expected to carry on the family name. Today, I have compassion for that role; but growing up, I was just pissed.

Jason and I had just finished a cross-country meet at Hargus Lake, and I needed to stop by a friend's house to figure out what we were wearing for spirit week. She and I were supposed to be "twinning" the next day at school, and I wanted to make sure we were still on the same page. This was before the day of cell phones, so she couldn't just snap me a pic of her outfit. Once at her house, I knew we couldn't just hang around. My parents had expectations, which included us getting home in a reasonable amount of time. We picked outfits in record time, and I was out the door within minutes. In the car, Jason said, "Let's try a new way home!"

"Are you sure about that?" I replied. It was getting dark, and I wasn't exactly an expert navigator.

"Yeah," he said. "Besides, I've been this way before. It will be a shortcut." There were no such things as shortcuts from my friend's house to our house. We were nearly thirty miles from our house, and even if we could cut a mile or two, we would have to do so by speeding down unmarked country roads. Unless we were going seventy miles an hour, we would not make it home any faster.

Driving home, listening to music, we were approaching a place in the road where we would have to turn. I thought, *Does Jason know where he is going?* As we approached the intersection, Jason didn't seem to be slowing down.

"Jason," I said, "there's a stop sign." I was pretty calm and was sure that he had heard me, but he didn't slow down. Very quickly, I began to feel uneasy about my brother's silence.

"Jason," I said. "Are you going to stop?" As we got closer, I realized this was no mere stop sign. There was a *T* in the road. If we didn't stop, we would find ourselves in the field. Still no response.

Finally, in what I can only describe as desperation, I yelled, *"Jason, you've got to stop!"* Too late. In his 1984 Olds, Jason ran the stop sign, plummeted over the bank, and dropped us into the field below.

We didn't get hit, and we didn't die. But we were both pretty sore when we realized we were no longer on the road and had crashed the car.

"How are we going to get out of here?" Jason asked. We were stuck in the mud and the wheels didn't look too stable.

"Let's try to get it out of the field," I said.

It took a while, but somehow we were able to get that car back onto the road and drive it twenty-five miles per hour the rest of the way home. We didn't realize it at the time, but my brother had bent the frame of the car, and there was no way we should have been able to drive it home. Both of us knew Mom and Dad wouldn't be happy. When we finally arrived home, we were late—really late on a school night—and we had destroyed my brother's car.

My brother had no problem throwing me under the bus—I mean the car. He was quick to tell my parents that the only reason he'd decided to go a "new way home" was because we had stopped at "my" friend's house first, and he'd wanted to make sure we didn't get home too late. It only seemed logical to him that the car accident was my fault.

I attempted to plead my case. "But, Jason," I whined, "I tried to get you to stop."

Yet, somehow, in what I can only describe as a masterful display of teenage manipulation, my brother convinced my parents that the car accident was all my fault. Somehow, in my parents' mind, I might as well have been behind the wheel. It was clear to me that there was a golden child in the family, and I was not it!

Look, David, I get it! I, too, wouldn't have been the one that Samuel was looking at with fondness. I didn't fit the leader profile either. My parents didn't even peg me as one to side with. David was the youngest, the runt, the little one whom no one took too seriously. Whether it was relegating him to tend sheep or asking him to wait on his two brothers, his family had made it clear that David had a job to do, and that was to serve his family, and especially the golden children, because their lives and legacy would be the life and legacy of the family.

But that's not what Samuel saw or what Jesse placed in front of the man of God. When Samuel asked for Jesse to gather all of his sons for worship and a meal, all the sons gathered— all except for David. Why? We can't really say. David had

> It's the uninvited one, the forgotten one, the labeled one, the outside one that God so readily anoints as leader of God's people and movement.

responsibilities; he had to tend the sheep. But wouldn't Jesse have someone else besides David watching after his flocks? Was David such a workaholic that he couldn't leave the field for just a few hours? Were the limitation prophecies that Jesse spoke over David so strong that David didn't consider himself part of the family?

David was uninvited to the most significant moment in his family's life. What happens when a man of God comes to your family's table and you are not even invited? It's a terrible feeling.

Uninvited

It wasn't until I was a teenager that I understood, for the first time in my family's history, the tension that existed between my paternal grandma and my mother. And I didn't help the tension. I was my Grandma Ruby's favorite, or at least I believed I was. In turn, I also let my mom know regularly where my allegiances stood. It's painful now to think about how stubborn and manipulative I could be and about how I had longed to stay in my grandma's good graces.

The realization dawned one Saturday afternoon, when my best friend Sarah and I had driven to my grandma's house to show off our looks. We had just readied ourselves for the high school homecoming dance. Julie, my little sister, had tagged along. When we came bounding into her house, my grandma seemed to share our enthusiasm about the dance. She complimented us on how nice we looked and encouraged us to have a good time. But soon people started pulling into the driveway. Family members were arriving with food in hand. When one of my relatives carried in a homemade cake, I realized what was going on. They were having a birthday party, and my family had not been invited. Although we lived just a mile up the road, for whatever reason, my dad and his family had not been asked to join. I was hurt and wanted to get out of there as quickly as possible.

My sister, who is five years younger than I am, didn't understand what was going on. "Julie," I said, "Sarah and I need to leave now if we are going to make it to the dance on time." Although we had hours before the start of the dance.

"No," Julie protested, "I'm staying! Look, Rachel, they are having a party."

I couldn't expect a ten-year-old to understand the family dynamics, so I said, "I am leaving, whether you stay or go."

Julie was persistent. "Grandma, can I stay with you?" she asked.

"Sure," Grandma replied.

And Sarah and I left. When I arrived home, I reported all that had happened. "Why weren't we invited?" I asked my dad.

"Rachel, it's complicated," he said.

Sad-mad, Dad grabbed his keys. "I am going to get your sister. You shouldn't have left her there!"

No, Dad, I shouldn't have, but we should have been invited.

Have you ever found yourself uninvited? Sometimes it's the family dinner table, the cafeteria at school, the lunchroom at work, or even the neighborhood barbecue. God created us all to be in relationship with the people around us. And when we find out that we are cut out or even rejected, it wounds us. It cracks our hearts and heads, and in response, sometimes we shield ourselves with deeper lies and half-truths: "Who needs them anyway? That didn't hurt me! Sticks and stones may break my bones, but words will never hurt me."

All of it is just plain bull. Words, actions, wh
and do—particularly, what our family does—c
identities.

Open Your Other Eyes

But in the middle of all that family relationship chaos, God
shows up and gives us a new way to see. With each son of
Jesse, God gave Samuel a new way of seeing and perceiving the
world. God reminded Samuel that God's view is the long view.
God saw, and sees, what you and I cannot see without God's
help. It wasn't the first born, the tall one, the strong one, the
one that made the most logical sense. It wasn't the one with
all the accomplishments or the one with the killer conquests.
Rather, it was the uninvited and forgotten one, the labeled one,
the outsider, that God so readily anointed as leader of God's
people and movement. Hear what I am saying! If you've ever
been labeled, rejected, mistreated, or uninvited, you are in
good company! God sees you! And God wants to use you and
your story for God's purposes.

God spoke to Samuel and said, "Not a single one of
these!" So, Samuel said to Jesse, "You got any more?" And Jesse
replied,

> *"There is still the youngest," Jesse answered. "He is
> tending the sheep." Samuel said, "Send for him; we will
> not sit down until he arrives." So he sent for him and had
> him brought in. He was glowing with health and had a
> fine appearance and handsome features. Then the LORD
> said, "Rise and anoint him; this is the one."*
>
> *1 Samuel 16:11-12*

God doesn't see the way we see. Our eyes are conditioned to look at features that we've been culturally trained to see as good, beautiful, strong, and anointed. And even though there is something about David's appearance that makes him contagious, it isn't that he stands head and shoulders above his brothers. I wonder if the contagious thing about David was his confidence in himself, in his God-given self-identity. Even when his family didn't affirm David's leadership, David continued to care for the family business. Whenever obstacles came David's way, David overcame them. What his family didn't know or couldn't know was that their limitation prophecies became the fuel for David's fire! Somehow, David had a deep connection to God. And with that deep connection to God, David was able to see himself and his potential as a leader of God's people.

So Samuel took the horn of oil and anointed him in the presence of his brothers, and from that day on the Spirit of the LORD came powerfully upon David. Samuel then went to Ramah.

1 Samuel 16:13

It's all good, right? David is going to be seen by others just as God saw him—as an anointed king. Right? But finding your fierce isn't about making sure everyone sees God's anointing on your life. Finding your fierce is about you seeing your anointing and living into it. And you've got to live into it even when others don't want you to. I would love to say that David's family stopped speaking limitation prophecies over David, but they didn't. Even after David was anointed by Samuel, the prophet of God, David showed up to care for his brothers who were serving in Israel's military, and they continued to speak limitations over him. While there, David overheard Goliath, a warrior giant, speak a curse over God and God's people. David wasn't having it. David knew God and knew God's love for God's people. David trusted God's leading. He asked the people around him, "What benefit is there to the man who kills Goliath?" The following scene ensued.

> When Eliab, David's oldest brother, heard him speaking with the men, he burned with anger at him and asked, "Why have you come down here? And with whom did you leave those few sheep in the wilderness? I know how conceited you are and how wicked your heart is; you came down only to watch the battle." "Now what have I done?" said David. "Can't I even speak?" He then turned away to someone else and brought up the same matter, and the men answered him as before. What David said was overheard and reported to Saul, and Saul sent for him.
>
> 1 Samuel 17:28-31

What was Eliab saying? Translation: "David, are you just here for the show? Are you looking to see someone killed? Who do you think you are? Get out of here, little brother!" David's family continued to refuse to see the God possibilities in David's life. But although his family didn't see him as a viable option for military leadership, David defeated the giant Goliath. What we know about David is that, more than being an underdog, he had radical trust in God and in God's anointing on his own life. You don't have to be the biggest, strongest, smartest, oldest, or youngest to be chosen and anointed by God. All you have to do is to trust God—to trust that God has placed fierce within you.

Brothers and sisters, I am inviting you on a journey. This journey is not for the faint of heart. Examine your life. Dive inward and comb through the hidden places of your life's stories. Forget the highlight reel—I want to hear it all. I want to see it all: the good, the bad, and the in-between. It's all part of your narrative.

We are human. We are messy. And our beautiful chaos does not limit God and God's ability to use it all to heal us and others from the inside out. But we have to give God space to work. Space to take our pain, pressures, and past and to shape it into God's glorious future.

Limitations Reversed

The same people who speak limitations over our lives can be the ones who make a way for us to experience our fierce. Over the years, I have learned to recognize with compassion the real-life limitations my own family members have experienced. At times, my family members have caused me great pain, and I have caused them pain as well. Yet I am able to see the gifts they have brought to my life. They have taught me to be fierce.

Last October, I was sitting in a leadership retreat for clergy, and the new Lead Pastor asked us to think about our Jesus stories. He said, "Think about your experience with Jesus. If Jesus wasn't an important part of your life, where would you be? Where would your family be?"

Instantly I thought of my mom and my Grandma Marie. Maybe my grandmother came to mind because it was her birthday and I had yet to call her, but certainly I thought of her faith. The women in my family have always been harbingers of Jesus's good news. In that moment I realized that, without their faithfulness, my journey to Jesus could have been, would have been, very different. So as soon as I arrived home, I called my Grandma Marie.

I could tell she was not expecting to hear my voice.

"Grandma," I said. "Can I talk with you about something?"

"Well sure, what is it?" she encouraged me to continue.

"I am not sure if you realize this, but because you had a relationship with Jesus, my mom had an opportunity to have a relationship with Jesus. And because Mom had a relationship with Jesus, that gave *me* an opportunity to have a relationship with Jesus. Your faith was a catalyst for generations of people to follow Jesus. Your faith has made an incredible difference in my life. I don't know if I have ever told you just how thankful I am for your faithfulness to Jesus and the church." I don't think that's what my grandma was expecting me to say that day, but something in what I said inspired her to share her story—her God story—with me again. I learned things about my grandmother that I never knew.

My grandmother reminded me that she had been fifteen when she married my thirty-three-year-old grandfather. She had given birth to five kids by the time she was twenty-five: my mom being the oldest. By 1969, she was divorced, drinking heavily, and desperately needing some hope. And one day, a little girl from the neighborhood knocked on her door and asked her to come to a church revival that week because it was her Sunday school class's turn to fill the pews. My grandmother didn't want to disappoint the little neighbor girl, so she said she would come. But after closing the door, panic set in. My grandma didn't have anything to wear to church. She said to me years later, "Rachel, I just couldn't go to church looking like I was looking, but then I remembered that Grandpa Bud had bought me a brand-new suit from Elder Beerman for Christmas that year. I thought to myself, *Maybe, just maybe, those church folks would accept me if I wore my new suit.*"

It pained me to realize that church folks have a reputation of creating conditions for people to experience Jesus's love—as though you've got to get yourself cleaned up, make sure you act or talk a certain way, or even totally change who you are to meet God. That's not how God works! God was already at work in my grandma's life. Long before that little girl knocked on the door, God was on the move. Like the prophet Samuel, this little girl carried with her the loving anointing of God. And although my grandmother wasn't going to be anointed king over God's people, she was going to be touched by the hand of God. And that touch, that anointing, would set her and future generations free!

And so on that day back in 1969, she went to the revival at South Perry United Methodist Church. That night, the preacher was a revivalist by the name of Charles Ragland, a Baptist minister who had a fire in his belly and a message on his lips. By the end of the night, my grandmother was ready to give her life to the Lord Jesus. When she came up to that altar, as she told me, "I was freed, freed from sin, freed from alcohol, and on a path that would change my life forever!"

By the time she finished sharing that day on the phone, I was crying, she was crying, and you could feel the power of the Holy Spirit right over the cell phone. I encouraged my grandmother to share her story with others. "Grandma," I said, "I needed to hear that! I believe there are people in your church, in your neighborhood, and frankly in our family who need to hear it too!" But more powerful than her story was the connection it had to my own story of finding Jesus.

What my grandmother couldn't have known was that Rev. Ragland would come back to South Perry United Methodist Church in March of 1991. (As a result of that day in 1969, I grew up attending South Perry.) What I didn't know was that the same preacher who'd preached that revival in 1969 was back at our little country church. At that time, I, too, felt lost. I was lost in darkness and depression even as an elementary-school kid. I had experienced pain in my life and I wanted more than anything just to sleep peacefully at night—at eleven years old! I would cry myself to sleep just praying that God would help me see what God saw in me. So when Rev. Charlie Ragland preached a message full of fierce passion, a message about the love of Jesus, a message telling me that I, too, could have that love, I went for it. I jumped at the chance to be filled with that kind of peace and joy. I remember being hesitant to go up to the altar. I didn't want to embarrass myself or my family. But then the fierce love of God flooded my body with such a force that I couldn't stay in my seat. I nearly ran to the altar! I knelt, and in what felt like a nanosecond, my grandma Marie, my mom, and the local pastor were crowded around me, helping me say yes to the fierce love of Jesus Christ.

Isn't that what it means to be human? We all are a combination of fierce life-giving words and self-limiting prophecies. Each day, you and I have a choice to make: Do we look for the fierce or do we seek out the limitations? Don't think for a moment that you are immune to speaking words of death over people, but also recognize your power. Realize your influence. You, my friend, have a story worth sharing. You have a fierce that the whole world wants to know about and to learn from. Don't hold back! Don't you dare hide. If we can't see it all, how on earth are we ever going to heal? We are on this journey together, and I pray that, together, we will find our fierce.

So What?

Reflect on your family of origin.

What "limitation prophecies" were spoken over you?

How are you still working through these? Have you allowed the labels and limitations to prohibit you from fiercely trusting forward?

How might perceived limitations get reimagined?

What will it take in this season of your life to find your fierce?

In Addition
What limitations have you spoken over your family: kids, grandkids, nieces, or nephews? How might you begin speaking a more positive future into their lives?

Prayer:
Open our eyes and help us see our lives, our families, our experiences the way that you see them, God. Give us and those we love the compassion and mercy to dive deep and look for the fuel that ignites our fierce.

∾ 2 ∾

THIN SLICE OF LIFE

*Go, gather together all the Jews who are in Susa, and
fast for me. Do not eat or drink for three days, night or
day. I and my attendants will fast as you do. When this
is done, I will go to the king, even though it is against the
law. And if I perish, I perish.*

(Esther 4:16)

Historically women have not gotten the best press in
Christianity. When you read through the Bible, you'll
notice that the Scriptures were written at a time when the culture
did not always treat women fairly. But God has always been God.
And Genesis 1:27 tells us that "God created humanity in God's
own image, in the divine image God created them, male and
female God created them" (CEB). All of us—men and women—
are created in God's image. Throughout history, God, through
the power of the Holy Spirit, superseded cultural limitations and
man-made boundaries, defied the norms of the day, and raised
fierce women to the forefront of the movement of God.

Now fellows, if you think this chapter has nothing to do
with you—think again! In a world of #metoo, you also have
the choice to promote the boys-will-be-boys club or join with

your partners in faith and promote a kingdom-of-God reality: "There is neither Jew nor Gentile, neither slave nor free, nor is there male and female, for you are all one in Christ Jesus" (Galatians 3:28). We are alive at a time when men and women of faith need a supernatural dose of fierce, and we must absolutely recognize and own the power we already have to make a difference in the world. We need to be partnered together!

I can't tell you the number of times people have pointed to the Scriptures 1 Timothy 2:12 ("I do not permit a woman to teach or to assume authority over a man; she must be quiet") or even 1 Corinthians 14:34 ("Women should remain silent in the churches. They are not allowed to speak, but must be in submission, as the law says") to declare that I have no business preaching the good news of Jesus or pastoring a church. To this, I always say, "What do you do with Mary Magdalene who was the first person to preach the good news of Jesus's resurrection?"

> Have you ever felt like you didn't have what it would take to move forward— face to face with being either the fool who believes the lies or the Jesus follower who risks choosing their fierce?

Let's think about that story. Jesus had just been resurrected and was standing at the tomb. Although, at first, Mary did not recognize Jesus, she finally realized that it was him and he was alive. Jesus said to Mary, "Do not hold on to me, for I have not yet ascended to the Father. Go instead to my brothers and tell them, 'I am ascending to my Father and your Father, to my God and your God'" (John 20:17).

Mary Magdalene was the first person to share with a group (of mostly men) that Jesus was alive and ascending into heaven! But yeah, we are talking about pulling Scriptures out of context to fit our understanding of how women and men should function in the church. We should be careful about that.

In fact, one summer evening my husband and I decided to go to a tent revival at a Baptist church in the mountains of North Carolina. I love Baptists, but not all of my Baptist brothers and sisters are affirming of women in ministry. My husband and I thought we knew what we were getting ourselves into; we assumed that we could participate in the singing portion of the revival celebration and then leave during the preaching if we needed to. This revival was different. There were multiple preachers and multiple singing groups. A preacher would preach for the length of a TED Talk, and then a group would come up to sing.

For six-plus hours this pattern went on: preach a little, then sing a little. And to my surprise, we were engaged in both the singing and the preaching. But then the host pastor came to the front of the tent and asked for all of the pastors in the audience to stand to be recognized. I did not stand—frankly, I knew better. But a couple of women were standing and talking to one another, one of them the pastor's wife, to which he said, "Ladies, I don't think you are pastors. You might want to sit down." They realized their social mistake, laughed, and then sat down. But that wasn't enough for the host pastor. He went on to say, "Well, I am glad we got that taken care of! Women are not pastors. In fact, if there is a woman here who thinks she is called to preach, she can go over to the little green structure located on the side of the tent and preach there!"

I wasn't paying much attention to what the host preacher was saying, but my husband was. He looked at me, horrified.

"Rachel," he said. "Do you realize what that so-called pastor just asked you to do?" Confused by his clear anger, I said, "No, what?"

"He just asked you to go and preach in the crapper!" The green structures at the side of the tent were portable toilets. Jon was fuming and would not let it go. He went to the front of the tent, talked to the host pastor, and then declared when he returned to our seat, "We are leaving. I've heard enough. Let's go!" And we did.

I am so grateful for my husband, my forever champion—but once again, a limitation prophecy was spoken over my life: "If you want to preach, preach in the crapper!"

Overcoming Fear

Heart-pounding, head-aching, gut-wrenching fear—that's what I was feeling. In January 2018, I found myself face to face with real-life fear and anxiety. I was stepping up and stepping out, doing something I had never done before. I had been invited to speak at the Resurrection Youth Conference in Pigeon Forge, Tennessee. With a thirty-year history and nearly ten thousand students and leaders in attendance, this would be the largest speaking opportunity of my life. I am mostly comfortable speaking to adults, but there is just something about that teenage angst and judgment that scares me to death. I love young people; it's just that I don't want them to think that I am lame, quirky, or just plain out of touch.

As I began preparing for Resurrection, fears began to crowd my mind and heart. And I started to hear it—you know, the lies that the enemy tries to tell us: "You can't do this. This is above your pay grade, you're going to make a fool of yourself. Who do you think you are, you're not even a youth pastor! Why don't you just play it safe and stay home?" Every day, for several weeks, the voices in my head would try to push me over the edge from fear into full-blown panic. And every day, I came face to face with the challenge: Will I be a fool and believe the lies or will I step out to find my fierce?

Ever felt that way before? Full of anxiety, riddled with gut-punching fear? The enemy filling your head and your heart with lies about who you think you are and what others might say about you? Have you ever felt like you didn't have what it would take to move forward—face to face with being either the fool who believes the lies or the Jesus follower who risks choosing their fierce?

Yes, I have, and yes, you have; we have all come face to face with fear verses fierce. And we are in good company! Men and women throughout the Bible have come face to face with the same choice—foolish fear or fierce faith—and they chose fierce. Because they chose fierce, God moved mightily through these men and women, changing lives and entire destinies. One of the most compelling examples of overcoming foolish fear is the story of Esther.

Recognize Your Power and Potential

The story of Esther begins with a young woman, orphaned as a girl, who hadn't yet recognized her power and her potential. She and her people, the Jews, were in exile. Exile was a form of political powerlessness. They'd spent years serving a foreign ruler, being oppressed, and hearing the lie that "all you Jews are a 'no people.'" Stripped of her cultural identity, parentless, and raised in a world that did not value women, Esther felt anything but powerful. But that's where life took a turn for Esther.

Xerxes was king of the Persian Empire, which stretched from Asia to the Mediterranean Sea. King Xerxes decided to hold a beauty contest because he was on the hunt for a new wife, a new queen. He had banished Queen Vashti because she wouldn't do what he wanted. The king had thrown a party, and after he and his guests had gotten pretty well intoxicated, King Xerxes requested that Queen Vashti expose herself in front of his drunken friends. (We are not the first ones to live in a #metoo world.) Queen Vashti reckoned the danger of the situation but hurt the king's ego with her refusal. When the king asked his powerful friends what he should do, they responded:

> "Queen Vashti has done wrong, not only against the king but also against all the nobles and the peoples of all the provinces of King Xerxes. For the queen's conduct will become known to all the women, and so they will despise their husbands and say, 'King Xerxes commanded Queen Vashti to be brought before him, but she would not come.' This very day the Persian and Median women of the nobility who have heard about the queen's conduct will respond to all the king's nobles in the same way. There will be no end of disrespect and discord."
>
> Esther 1:16-18

In the middle of this political and relational mess, Esther entered the story. Esther had a gift—she was kind and beautiful. Esther had been raised by her cousin Mordecai, who had a glimpse of how God might use this gift. He saw potential in Esther and signed her up for the contest. The contest included twelve months of beauty treatments and a competition, and at the end of the year, Esther won the competition.

> *Now the king was attracted to Esther more than to any of the other women, and she won his favor and approval more than any of the other virgins. So he set a royal crown on her head and made her queen instead of Vashti. And the king gave a great banquet, Esther's banquet, for all his nobles and officials. He proclaimed a holiday throughout the provinces and distributed gifts with royal liberality.*
>
> *Esther 2:17-18*

I know that an ancient beauty pageant does not sound like women's empowerment, but stay with me here. Esther won and became queen of the Persian Empire. But until now, she had been a nobody, an orphan. Esther had no parents, no power, and no potential. But then God stepped into Esther's life.

Ever feel like a nobody? Ever feel like Esther: no family, no power, and no potential? I remember the first time I felt like a nobody, limited by my gender and social status. I was in middle school and nominated for a leadership immersion experience. I would be traveling to a place where a classmate of mine and I would be poured into as future leaders. Our school selected one boy and one girl for the trip. I was honored, excited, and ready for the opportunity. But then one day, the principal came to me and said I wouldn't be going after all. As it turned out, only one person could be nominated from each school, so only my classmate would be going. At first I didn't understand. I'm quite sure I shed a few tears.

While I was feeling sorry for myself, someone in the office noticed my distress. Attempting to be helpful, she said, "Oh,

Rachel don't be upset. You can't go because we could only send one student. We are sending Adam. He has more leadership potential than you do because he is a boy." Because he is a boy? For the first time in my life, I was told that there was a ceiling to my potential. I didn't choose that ceiling, I didn't ask for it, but society created it for me. And in that moment, I felt like a nobody.

I'm sure I am not alone. We all have those moments in our lives where we think we don't have power. We can point back to times when we believed we didn't have potential. Maybe your defining moment came when you didn't make the basketball team. Maybe you were limited by someone who told you, "You're from the wrong side of the tracks." Perhaps you were bullied or told you weren't college material. But whatever happened, that experience limited your person, your potential, and your power! But then God stepped into your life.

When I read through the pages of the Bible, I see that God gravitates to the nobodies. God sees us, God hears us, and God promises to use us in power-filled ways. That's Esther's story! God recognized the power and potential in this young woman. God chose her. And, as we'll see, God used her to save God's people. And God wants to do the same in your life and in mine! Do you see your potential? Do you know your power? The power to step into the next dimension of your God journey? The power to take that new job, that new promotion, to go for that scholarship? The power to start that ministry that God has laid on your heart? Recognize your potential. Don't ever fall into the trap of thinking that you don't have any power.

Surrender Your Fear

Even Esther, queen of Persia, struggled to embrace her power. But Mordecai wouldn't allow her to shrink down or bail out. The Jews—God's people and Esther's people—were in a world of trouble. Her own husband, King Xerxes, had been persuaded to sign an edict to annihilate every Jew in the Persian Empire, and Mordecai was sick over it. He was weeping, wailing, and sitting at the king's gate making a scene. And even though Esther wants Mordecai to stop the commotion, Mordecai refuses. "No, Esther! I will not stop, I will not stop while the very existence of our people is threatened." Mordecai wanted her to confront the king. But Esther was worried and anxious. She was filled with fear. She fully understood the strict, harsh rules of royalty. And she said to her cousin Mordecai,

> *"All the king's officials and the people of the royal provinces know that for any man or woman who approaches the king in the inner court without being summoned the king has but one law: that they be put to death unless the king extends the gold scepter to them and spares their lives. But thirty days have passed since I was called to go to the king."*
>
> *Esther 4:11*

In others words, "I can't, Mordecai! I can't do that! If I go, there's a really good chance that the king could have me killed. He could get rid of me just like he got rid of Queen Vashti. And besides, it's been a month since my husband, the king, even wanted to see my face! I can't take the risk!" Esther was terrified. But Mordecai challenged her fear. He would not hold back.

> *"Do not think that because you are in the king's house you alone of all the Jews will escape. For if you remain silent at this time, relief and deliverance for the Jews will arise from another place, but you and your father's family will perish. And who knows but that you have come to your royal position for such a time as this?"*
>
> Esther 4:13-14

"Esther, the time is now! Don't wait! The very lives of the people around you depend on it."

Hey, reader, the time is now! Don't wait! The very lives of the people around you depend on you. You've got to surrender your fear. You've got to surrender your fear and apply for that new job. You've got to surrender your fear and end that unhealthy relationship. You've got to surrender and let your kid move out of state. You've got to surrender and take a risk on a healthier lifestyle. Stop living in fear, for who knows that you have come to your position for such a time as this!

Esther was living in a state of fear. It was fear that drove her to silence her cousin Mordecai. It was fear that kept her hiding her identity. It was fear that told her she couldn't when the existence of her people was in jeopardy. It was fear! Fear can be such a debilitating force in our lives: it's what keeps us from standing up and stepping out! It's fear of failing, but at times it's fear of succeeding! I find that there are times in my life that I realize if I do this thing, it may open doors that I am not ready to be opened. What if my life gets more hectic? What if my territory gets larger? What if I get that new promotion? What if my influence is expanded and I haven't thought through my next steps?

Fear has this crazy ability to keep us from becoming the women and men God created us to be. Those limitation prophecies have a way of playing over and over in our minds, and before we know it, we are paralyzed. We become stuck in our careers, paralyzed in our relationships, and unable to navigate the tough stuff of friendships, and we settle for a less-than-full version of life. We are afraid. And when face to face with fear, you and I, like Esther, have a decision to make: stay afraid for life or surrender our fear! Esther knew Mordecai was right. It was her moment to stand up and lead. "Who knows Esther, but that you have come to your royal position for such a time as this!" Esther chose courage. She surrendered her fears, summoned her faith, and handed her future and the future of her people over to God. She chose fierce.

Running Down Fear

We all can point to moments in our lives when fear got the best of us. I grew up with a strong desire to be a star athlete. I wasn't bad; I just wasn't a star. But I worked hard. And so senior year of high school, I found myself on the cusp of finishing in the top ten at the Mid-State League Cross-Country meet, and I was slated to make the all-league cross-country team. I remember being really aware of my placement; and as I neared the finish line, I was about to realize my accomplishment. But suddenly, out of the corner of my eye, I noticed a runner coming up from behind me. If she outsprinted me, I wouldn't make the all-league team. I wasn't tired and could have beaten her, but in that moment I panicked. Riddled with the fear of losing this foot race, my legs began to feel like cement, and fear slowed me down. I watched as my hopes for being an all-league runner were dashed at the finish line.

It's a great metaphor for life, isn't it? We've done the work, we've come prepared to the presentation, the pulpit, the platform, only to allow fear to get the best of us so that we come up short at the finish line.

But fierce can grow in our lives. If we didn't grab onto fierce the first time, there will be many more opportunities. Freshman year of college cross-country, I trained and prepared and, through meditation, I strengthened my mental fierce. Meditation is not only great for the soul; it's also an incredible way to strengthen the mind and, in the process, tell the body what it will do. "Mind over matter!" Once again, I found myself at the end of the season at the league meet, now in college-conference participation, and I was determined to finish strong. The same exact scenario began to take place—I could see the finish line and I was about to be awarded an all-conference position. Then out of the corner of my eye, I noticed a girl working to run past me in the final stretch. But I said to myself, "Not this time," and refused to go down without a fight. Fear wasn't going to beat me and neither would this young woman. I pumped my arms, relaxed my jaw, and kicked it into high gear. That day, fear didn't win—my fierce did.

Fiercely Trust Forward

Esther also faced an opponent. But for her, it was a matter of life and death. The oppressive Haman was determined to annihilate the Jews. He tricked King Xerxes into signing an edict and, in the process, the king signed away the lives of his wife and her people. It was a death sentence. Esther had every right to be afraid.

Have you ever found yourself in a situation that warranted real-life fear? Fear is a natural emotion. There are moments in our lives when we are going to be afraid. Fear is not the absence of fierce; rather, fierce puts our natural fear in its rightful place. So how does Esther overcome fear with so much at stake? Fierce trust! Esther trusted in her God.

> *"Go, gather together all the Jews who are in Susa, and fast for me. Do not eat or drink for three days, night or day. I and my attendants will fast as you do. When this is done, I will go to the king, even though it is against the law. And if I perish, I perish."*
>
> *Esther 4:16*

When Esther did not trust her own power, she placed her trust in God. She asked all of the Jewish people to join her in prayer and fasting for three days. If you've never heard of fasting, it means they chose not to eat in order to be focused on listening for the voice of God. They didn't want to be distracted by food or by prepping for meals but wanted to be closely in touch with the very power of God. Esther wanted to fast because she wanted to be in alignment with the movement of the Holy Spirit in her life and the lives of God's people. Once Esther surrendered her fear, she made room for fierce and faith-filled trust. Esther declared, "If I die, I die!" and in so doing, she proclaimed her faith in God. This was no suicide mission. This was not "I don't care." This was "I will be who God calls me to be even if it takes my life." This is fiercely trusting forward.

Fierce Trust

I remember it like it was yesterday. I was talking on the phone with a church leader about my call into ministry. I was a year and a half into the multi-year process of becoming an ordained pastor, and he wanted to make me start over.

> The funny thing about fear is that it's not one and done. Fear has a regular return policy.

"Rachel," he said, "you have skipped a few steps, and although you've worked really hard, the process is the process." It all seemed like a lot of spiritual red tape to me. I'm not sure he meant to, but he spoke a limitation prophecy over me. He had asked me if I was planning to go to seminary and I said, "Yes. I want to go to Duke Divinity School at Duke University."

"Oh, Rachel," he replied, "that's a really hard school to get into and academically rigorous. I really think you need to consider going somewhere else. We can talk about it next month when you meet with the rest of the board."

"Really? Okay," I said. And I finished that phone conversation filled with the kind of determination that wells up inside me whenever people tell me, "Rachel, you can't!" I was frustrated, and I channeled my frustrated to fierce. I knew I had heard God say that I was called to be a pastor, to be a preacher, and to be in full-time ministry. I had a fierce trust in the call of God on my life.

Fast forward two months. There I was at the table with the ordination board. These leaders knew the small church that I had grown up in, they knew the demographics of my hometown, and they thought they knew me. Determined to prove them wrong with an extra dose of attitude, I showed up in the most countrified farm-girl outfit I could muster the courage to wear and still be respectful: denim skirt, elbow-length hair pulled up on the top in a bun, and a nice fall sweater that I am sure my mom purchased at Tractor Supply. You see, I was from the Hocking Hills, a rural community in Appalachian Ohio, born into a family with limited education. Although my family worked hard, very few even ventured to have dreams beyond the boundaries of Hocking County. To this group of church leaders, I looked like I came from a thin slice of life, so they put me into a category and labeled me accordingly.

We began with small talk around the table, and soon they were asking me about my Jesus journey. I began sharing about my love for Jesus and the church. How I had felt the hand of God leading me into pastoral and preaching ministry. "My husband, Jon, and I prayed for me to get a scholarship to go to seminary, so that we wouldn't have more student loans to pay. We visited Duke, and after our visit believed stronger than ever that we were called to move to Durham, North Carolina. I am looking for a seminary for students who love the church and that is academically rigorous," I said, waiting to get everyone's undivided attention. "So, when Duke's admissions director called and told me that I got in with a full ride, Jon and I were elated!" I declared.

There was an audible gasp in the room. The board chair's eyes were as big as saucers. They were shocked. Later, when the meeting had turned into a debate about the theology of Soren Kierkegaard, the leader stopped everyone and turned to me. "We are sorry," he said. "Clearly, we had no idea who you were. We thought we knew you, but we didn't. We see the Jesus in you, we sense your call, and we want to help you in your journey. You don't have to start over."

That day, I walked into a room of adversaries and walked out with a new group of advocates. Often in our lives, we expect other people to change their perceptions of who we are. When we are labeled, judged, oppressed, or misunderstood, we expect the people around us to immediately change their attitudes with little or no work. I wish I could say that human beings are full of grace and generally assume the best in others, but usually that's not the case. Maybe it's because we are too busy with our own grab-bag of fear to notice the fierce in others. Or perhaps it's because life has made us a little hard or crusty around the edges. Whatever the case, usually it takes a cosmic knock upside the head to realize that, no, this man or woman is operating out of fierce. This is why we should not speak a limitation prophecy over others' lives but rather speak words of life-giving encouragement. Encouragement is free and may just be one of the most profound forms of fierce that we can share with one another. When we share fierce through encouragement, we are telling ourselves and the world that we are secure in who we are and in who God has created us to be. Fierce trust propels us all forward!

Brothers and sisters, the funny thing about fear is that it's not one and done. Fear has a regular return policy. Most of the time, we are operating out of some form of fear. And what I know is that while we will frequently be afraid, we must choose to trust forward. Trust that God is going to show up again and again and again. Trust the promise that God has spoken over your life: "And surely I am with you always, to the very end of the age" (Matthew 28:20b). God never promised a fearless life, but rather promised God's own powerful presence in those moments of fear. So, trust that God will provide you with the power you need to step into fierce.

God used Esther to save her people. Esther trusted God. And in the end, King Xerxes delivered God's people from the very hands of the enemy that had sought to destroy them.

King Xerxes replied to Queen Esther and to Mordecai
the Jew, "Because Haman attacked the Jews, I have given
his estate to Esther, and they have impaled him on the pole
he set up. Now write another decree in the king's name in
behalf of the Jews as seems best to you, and seal it with the
king's signet ring—for no document written in the king's
name and sealed with his ring can be revoked."

Esther 8:7-8

Esther, the queen of Persia, had fierce trust in the face of life-threatening fear.

And that takes us back to the youth conference. Evil wanted to convince me that I wasn't capable of leading or being used mightily by God. "Rachel, who do you think you are? You can't possibly do this! You are going to fail!" But I trusted forward. In the weeks leading up to the conference, I prayed 2 Timothy 1:7, saying, "God you did not give me a spirit of fear, but of power, of love, and of self-discipline." I didn't just pray it once—I prayed it over and over and over again. I was afraid, but fear didn't keep me from stepping into fierce and doing what I believed God was calling me to do. Jon, Adeline (my oldest daughter), and I drove down to Tennessee, and on multiple occasions, I said to them, "I can't believe I am doing this! I am not even a youth pastor. Who thought that this was a good idea?" And because he is and will always be my champion, Jon replied, "You were made for this. Do not be afraid!"

He was right. What happened that weekend exceeded all my expectations. Friday, when I stepped onto the platform, I said, "Okay, Jesus, I trust you." And we were on our way. On the Saturday night of the youth conference, hundreds of kids gave their lives to Jesus, and on Sunday morning following my last message, a youth leader approached me and said, "Before this trip two of my girls had been unsure of their faith in Jesus, but God, through you, has lit them on fire. They are different. They saw you on the platform, and for the first time they are dreaming of new possibilities for their lives. They have never heard a woman preach. And now they too are sensing the call of God to go into full-time ministry." When given the opportunity to come forward on Sunday morning, 238 students signed up to explore a call into full-time ministry! It was one of those heaven-meets-earth moments in my life, and I was honored to be a part of what God was already doing in the room.

My being on that platform was a miracle of God, but being on that platform was not really about me. God wants to raise up a generation of young women and young men who will lead the church into its future, and I was excited to discover that this was part of my call: *to be used by God to spiritually pave the way for this next generation to become the Spirit-filled leaders that God desires.* That moment became a catalyst in my life to help me recognize that it was high time that I start giving my life and my ministry away. It was time to intentionally pour God's best in me into God's best for others. Although as a much younger pastor I dreamed of having the opportunity to be a resource to teens, I realize now is the time.

In the end, I was grateful for the chance to develop my own fear into fierce in order to pour my life into the lives of a new generation of fierce Jesus followers.

So What?

For each one reading today, dare to recognize your own power. Dare to realize your unique potential. Fully surrender your fear and fiercely trust forward. You and I have been created in the very image of God, and God wants to use our very best selves to transform the small thinking and brokenness of this world into resurrected life. Here's the deal, folks—we are all going to die. Not one of us will get out of this life alive! The question is not, Will you die? The question is, Will you actually live? Will you live a life of fierce trust?

And to the women reading this book . . . sisters! Don't shrink back, do not limit your potential, don't quiet your voice, and certainly don't think that just because you are a woman that you can't be used by God: in the name of Jesus Christ, find your fierce!

When you think back over your life, can you pinpoint moments of fear?

Who in your life spoke limitation prophecies over you? How did they shape your perception of yourself: in school, at home, in your career, or in your future choices?

When did you first realize that you needed to find your fierce? How did you respond to the situation?

Who in your life started as an adversary and turned into an advocate?

Name the adversaries in your life. Can they be transformed into advocates? If not, why do these folks have space in your life?

3

CONFESSIONS OF A MEAN GIRL

*Your beauty should not come from outward adornment,
such as elaborate hairstyles and the wearing of gold jewelry
or fine clothes. Rather, it should be that of your inner self,
the unfading beauty of a gentle and quiet spirit, which
is of great worth in God's sight. For this is the way the
holy women of the past who put their hope in God used to
adorn themselves. They submitted themselves to their own
husbands, like Sarah, who obeyed Abraham and called
him her lord. You are her daughters if you do what is right
and do not give way to fear.*

1 Peter 3:3-6

These words about unfading beauty and quiet strength seem more like an advertisement for a women's deodorant commercial than a power-packed definition of fierce. Couple that with words like *obedience* and *submission,* and we've got the makings of a regular march for women's rights on our hands. But before I dismiss the words of 1 Peter and the description of Sarah, our grandmother in the faith, as ancient prose without merit for a twenty-first-century context, I want to dig deep. My desire is to uncover the fierce within each of us: so here I am, calling all wallflowers, Rambo types, social icons, would-be-if-they-could-be hermits, and those of us who wear each of those labels depending on the day. Come with me, dive deep with me, and together, let's talk about fierce.

The gift of fierce can become a life force. It's given to us with the intent of helping us find our true child-of-God selves. But let's talk about when our own breed of fierce fails us. When muddled with our humanness, fierce can come out sideways. In the personal hunt for our fierce, we can weaponize our boldness and harm people around us. People whom we call friends and allies can become enemies and victims of our forceful fierce. And if we are not careful, we can lose our superhero and heroine status and become the same villain we were so desperately trying to fight.

I Am Wonder Woman

When I was a kid, I sported a Wonder Woman costume for Halloween. I grew up in the 1980s when most store-bought costumes consisted of the same full-size onesie that tied up in the back. The box sets came with a plastic mask. They were painful, and the mask's little rubber straps cut into the skin on the sides of your face when you put it on. And since our trick-or-treating seemed to last forever, comfortable these costumes were not. But one fateful Halloween, I received a Wonder Woman leotard. Its style was impeccable, its comfort a perfect ten; there was no plastic mask, no awkward jumpsuit. Soon this Halloween costume became my wardrobe of choice. I wore it every day. Did you know that leotards go with pants, with a skirt, over a bathing suit, or under a dress? It became a part of me: I wore it again and again and again and again until I refused to wear anything else. I'm sure after a while it wasn't looking so great, and I can't imagine the smell. Finally, my mom got so frustrated with me she decided to hide the leotard. My mother wasn't great at hiding stuff from my siblings and me. We lived in a small house, where it didn't take long for curious and mischievous kids to find her hiding places.

Knowing this, I went on the hunt. While mom was out working in the yard, I went into her bedroom. Was it in my parents' closet? Nope, not there. What about under their bed? No, but I found some toys that my brother and I had been fighting over. What about behind the headboard? Bingo— found it. In my young mind, if my mom refused to work creatively on her hiding skills, then she must have wanted me to find it. The next morning, I came bounding out of my room dressed as Wonder Woman. When I put that costume on, I felt like I could do anything. My older brother, Jason, couldn't pick on me, and the neighbor boys down the road couldn't harass me. With Wonder Woman covering every square inch of my body, I was unstoppable. Where did all of that awe for Wonder Woman come from? I wanted to be superhero. We kids grew up with no cable television and three channels of TV fuzz, but somehow I managed to realize that Wonder Woman was fierce: she was strong, beautiful, and courageous. She knew how to fight for the right stuff. As an adult, I recognize the influence Wonder Woman has over us, and it is not just because of her lasso of truth or her projectile tiara. When we look at superheroes like Wonder Woman or Captain America, we see a picture of ourselves. What if we, too, could fight for peace, justice, and love in the world? What if we could have superpowers that reviled all those supervillains in our lives? It was and is possible for us to fight for the right stuff. Yes, we can!

But being a superwoman or a superman isn't just about power, strength, and the ability to fight the bad guys or gals. It starts way before that, and it's about our pictures: the real-life pictures of what it means to be a hero. Lucky for us, God has left us some pretty cool and amazing pictures of heroes and heroines in the Bible.

One of those heroines is Sarah. Sarah is pretty significant in our story. She is one of the grandmothers of our faith. Sarah is a Bible superhero, but just because she is a superhero doesn't mean that she was perfect. Sometimes we imagine that people in the Bible never struggled with faith, belief, love, or life. Even when we read about their flaws in detail, we tend to spiritualize those flaws, make them go away, or sometimes just refuse to believe they existed. We think, *There's no way that people celebrated for their faithfulness have tattered pasts.* But they are and they did. Sometimes people attempt to boil faith and faithful living down to an expectation of personal and professional perfection. As though everyone has to have it all figured out from the beginning: no missteps, no mistakes, no mess-ups. It's a broken perspective that sometimes creates jealousy or even a spiritual caste system that includes religious elites. And so, in that regard, Sarah's story is curious and maybe even refreshing. Sarah is a real-life work in progress. She doesn't start her journey as the heroine of faith. Although known for her faithfulness to Abraham and her inner beauty, Sarah actually began her journey with a mean spirit. That's right— the mother our faith started out as a "mean girl." She used her fierce as force, and it nearly destroyed both her and her husband's lives in the process.

Confessions of a Mean Girl

I have a true and horrible confession to make. When I was in seventh grade, I did probably one of the meanest things I've ever done in my life. Let me tell you something about middle school. When I think about what hell might be like, I think about middle school. Just plain torture! Every second dealing with wondering if your armpits smell, and then walking into a classroom wearing a flowered shirt but then noticing all the people in the room are wearing flannels. It's a total freak-out moment. It's years of wondering, *Do I belong? Do I fit in? Am I going to survive this?* If you happen to be a middle-school kid reading this book, trust me: you will make it, you are strong, and I am rooting for you! We all are rooting for you!

Life if full of changes in middle school. Most students are changing buildings, bodies, and buddies. With all that change comes a limited grasp of personal identity. *Who am I now?* And when this change meets hormones, it can be a recipe for disaster. But it can also be a recipe for growth. I changed a lot in middle school. Some change was good. Some change was not so good.

In elementary school, I was friends with a girl called Jessie (not her real name). Jessie was part of my elementary-school posse. Our core group ate lunch together, sat on the bench during gym class together, and palled around at sixth-grade adventure camp together. We were inseparable, or at least I thought we were inseparable. But middle school brought with it hundreds of new students from three other elementary schools, and new people meant new friends. Besides, we now had choices: we could choose what classes to take, what activities to participate in, and even what to eat at lunch. For the first time in my life, I could have a milkshake for lunch and no one could tell me no. It was glorious! So maybe I had a milkshake every day for the first three weeks, but who can blame me? It was my first experience of real-life choices.

In elementary school, Jessie and I were known as the chubby kids. When I look back at pictures, I realize that we weren't that big; just really hard on ourselves. But we were definitely treated as chubby kids. For example, we were not expected to run the mile for the Presidential Physical Fitness Test. Jessie and I were asked to be on certain teams for tug-of-war. And we had the benefit of getting anyone's extra snacks that they didn't want to eat for lunch.

The summer before middle school, I knew I needed to gain some healthy habits to curb my rapid weight gain. I loved sports, and my first love was basketball, so I went to basketball camp at Rio Grande College. I wasn't used to being away from home. Soon I became homesick and found myself talking with girls from other schools. I began a conversation with a future teammate. We talked about seventh-grade volleyball. "Are you trying out?" she asked.

"I think I am," I said. "But I don't know much about volleyball. I've played in gym class, but I am not very good."

"Well, I am thinking about running cross-country," she said.

"What's that?" I asked. I had never heard of cross-country.

"Running," she replied.

"Like, for fun?"

"Yeah, and you don't even have to try out."

That's exactly what I needed to hear—no tryouts, no not making the team, no rejection, everyone is in. That day I was determined to sign up for cross-country. I was not a good runner, but knew it would help me get in shape for basketball. I soon discovered that running helped with discipline, and then healthy discipline bled into every area of my life, including what I ate. By spring of seventh grade, I had lost a significant amount of weight and was within a healthy weight range for a thirteen-year-old.

One day, Jessie walked by me during study hall. I looked at her with judgment. In my mind, she hadn't changed: same look, same weight, same old Jessie. I told the person next to me what I was thinking. "Can you believe what she is wearing? Someone should tell her not to wear that!"

"Why not you?" the girl said. "You all were friends. Just tell her what you think!"

Yeah, I thought to myself. *Why not me?* I began to convince myself that by saying something, I would be acting out of fierce. After all, people knew me for my confidence and for standing up for the right stuff (most of the time). So of course I should be fierce and tell Jessie what I thought. Then, masked in this bent form of boldness, I began to write my thoughts. And what started out as friendly concern quickly turned into a mean, hateful, judgmental note. It was awful. Although I can remember some of the things I wrote, I am too embarrassed and ashamed to tell you everything. In a nutshell, I took it upon myself to tell Jesse she was overweight and needed to do something about it. When I think about the stuff I wrote in that note, I want to cry, not just because it was mean, but also because I realize that all I was doing was masking my own insecurity and desperation to fit in. And fierce became my weapon of choice. Further, I didn't just write the note; with smug confidence, I handed it to her.

"Here," I said, "you need to read this."

Soon Jessie and a friend paid me a little visit in science class. I don't know how they got permission to get me out of class, but the teacher dismissed me into the hallway. There we were, Jessie clearly upset, and her friend asking me how I was capable of such blatant meanness.

"Did you write this?" she asked. "This is cruel! I thought you were her friend."

I backpedaled—so much for force fierce.

"I was just joking," I said. "I didn't intend to hurt your feelings, Jessie."

We stood there in awkward silence.

"I am sorry I even wrote the letter," I said finally.

We exchanged a few more words and then headed back to class. I was sorry, but my pathetic apology seemed just enough to calm the friend and keep Jessie from getting me into trouble. Besides, the damage had already been done.

Summer break came and went. When we arrived back at school in the fall, the entire eighth grade class was gathered in the cafeteria. A warm buzz of laughter and excitement filled the room. I began looking for my friends when I noticed a girl I hadn't seen before.

"Who's that new girl?" I asked a friend.

"Oh, that's not a new girl," she told me. "That's Jessie."

Jessie was unrecognizable. She was thin—real thin. I didn't realize it was possible to lose that much weight in a couple of months over the summer. Students were crowding around Jessie saying things like, "Wow, it's you, Jessie!" Boys were calling out, "Looking good!" Jessie radiated a shy confidence that seemed both mysterious and delightful at the same time. This was all new for her. Although part of me was happy for Jessie, there was something sad about the way she looked. Like many middle schoolers, Jessie exhibited all the signs of an eating disorder. As I watched her walk through the room, hallowing conviction came over me. Later, I would find out that she struggled with eating disorders, and I couldn't help but think that my note to her had been a contributing factor. I had used my fierce as a weapon, and Jessie's self-image had taken a blow.

Truth is, I struggled with my own body image and, somehow, in middle school, I believed the lie that if I made someone else feel bad about themselves, I would feel better about myself. I didn't feel better, not when I gave Jessie the note, not when she read the note, and certainly not at that eighth-grade gathering when I saw the real-life results of my fierce-forced actions. I am certain I am not alone in my experience. Some of us haven't gotten over those negative pictures of ourselves that were seared in our minds in middle school!

That said, distorted body image is not exclusive to girls and women. There is an alarming rise of incidents of distorted body image and eating disorders among men. According to the National Eating Disorders Association, nearly 10 million males will be affected by eating disorders within their lifetime.[1] And it's no wonder, when we live in a culture where we are bombarded with the message that thinner is better. But it raises the question, How thin is thin enough?

A few years ago, I ran across an article about the teen clothing giant Abercrombie & Fitch. Abercrombie's former CEO, Mike Jeffries, was clear that he only wanted beautiful, thin, young people in his clothing. Listen to what he had to say: "In every school there are the cool and popular kids, and then there are the not-so-cool kids. Candidly, we go after the cool kids. We go after the attractive all-American kid with a great attitude and a lot of friends. A lot of people don't belong [in our clothes], and they can't belong. Are we exclusionary? Absolutely."[2] How cruel is this statement? Yet many people operate within this narrative. It's the prevailing narrative of middle school and, sadly, is one that some people never grow out of.

My mom used to say, "Rachel, it isn't what's on the outside, but what is on the inside that counts." Well, Mom, that is really easy to say, but we live in a culture of comparison, and you don't have to be a middle schooler to feel its pain. Whether you were bullied or, like me and Mr. Jeffries, bullied others, using a false fierce to make yourself feel better never gets the job done. Humans were created to be in life-giving relationships with one another. We were never created for the comparison game.

Comparison Game

Fierce turned into a destructive force for Sarah. Still, Sarah was a Bible heroine. She followed her husband, Abraham, to a place neither of them had ever seen with their own eyes. Can you imagine? Your spouse asks you to leave everything you have ever known to go to a place he or she has never seen. And by the way, you have to leave your family behind and hope that, as you take this nearly five-hundred-mile journey on foot, you make it there alive. In Genesis, we read that God asked Abraham and Sarah to travel from Ur to Canaan—with the promise that they would be the mother and father of God's people:

> *"I will make you into a great nation, and I will bless you; I will make your name great, and you will be a blessing. I will bless those who bless you, and whoever curses you I will curse; and all peoples on earth will be blessed through you."*
>
> *Genesis 12:2-3*

They went because they trusted God. At least they trusted God enough to pack up their bags and leave. And Sarah trusted and believed God, embracing the promise, until people started to talk. Because, while one might think that, after their act of seemingly blind obedience, Abraham and Sarah would immediately start having babies. But that's not what happened. Not within a "reasonable" timeframe. After twenty-five years— yes, twenty-five long years—Abraham and Sarah still had no children. And I can imagine that people were starting to talk.

"She's too old now!"

"Can you believe she came all this way for nothing!"

"God must have forgotten her!"

"How is Abraham ever going to be the Father of Nations? Sarah can't even give him one son!"

People are cruel, and Sarah started to believe the lies.

Did you know that doubt is an integral part of the comparison game? If there is no doubt, there is no game. New is fun for me. I have no problem starting something new: a new job, a new exercise routine, or even a move to a new place. But once I start the new thing, it's the doubt that keeps me guessing. I believe this is what happened to Sarah. She began to wonder, "Has God forgotten me? What kind of wife am I that I can't even give my husband a son?"

> Unhealthy criticism and limitation prophecies distort our image of ourselves and leave us grasping for any and all forms of life.

Childbearing was an integral part of a woman's identity in the Old Testament world. Long before a clinical understanding of fertility and reproduction, women were judged by their ability or inability to produce heirs for a family's inheritance. Mothering was a woman's job, mothering was her identity, and mothering was what God promised her to do. So, after twenty-five long years and a heavy dose of doubt, Sarah took matters into her own hands.

Hagar was Sarah's servant girl (the actual Hebrew word used in the text is *slave*). Sarah asked Abraham to sleep with Hagar so that "they" could have a baby. When I read this story in the Bible, I am full of trash talk and smack. I want to give both Sarah and Abraham a piece of my mind. I get that I am living in a different culture with different standards, but . . . *Abraham, really? And Sarah, your life is about to become as predictable as any plot on a daytime soap opera.* Yet Sarah believed that she could force her future—force her fierce. Sarah used Hagar to get what she thought she wanted. But in the end, it did not turn out the way Sarah expected.

Abraham slept with Hagar, and Hagar became pregnant and gave birth to Ishmael. Ishmael was a real game-changer. Not only did this episode make Sarah jealous of Hagar and Ishmael, but she began to believe the lie that she was no longer a part of God's promise. Doubt, insecurity, anger, and jealousy were all signs that Sarah no longer believed God's promise.

Never believe the lie that you are not part of God's promise. What happens to us when we begin to believe lies about ourselves?

"You are not good enough!"

"You can't get the job done."

"You are a failure!"

"Your hair, your abs, your teeth, your clothes, your calves, your [fill in the blank]—they just aren't good enough."

When we believe those lies, we tend to become depressed, bitter, and angry. We are robbed of happiness and joy. The darkness seeps deep within our souls and smothers any notion of inner self or inner boldness that we once had.

It doesn't take much for one to become doubtful and discouraged about what we see in ourselves. It doesn't take much for us to doubt God's promises over us. Even though I know that I am a beloved daughter of God, I have to see just a few hateful comments on my Facebook page or a "nasty gram" in my email inbox, and soon I am in full-fledged doubt. *Can I really do this? Is it possible? Am I good enough?* In those moments, I want to give people a piece of my mind, drop the microphone, and go live off the grid.

Unhealthy criticism and limitation prophecies distort our image of ourselves and leave us grasping for any and all forms of life. Sarah was grasping and decided to place Hagar into her husband's hands. But when Hagar became pregnant, the pain and pressure were too much for Sarah. And she compared herself to a much younger Hagar. The pain, doubt, darkness, and despair led her to treat Hagar, a fellow human, mother to her stepson, with bitterness and contempt. And what did Abraham do about it? The unthinkable: Abraham permitted Sarah to do anything she wished to Hagar. The Bible does not give us details but merely states, "Then Sarai mistreated Hagar; so she fled from her" (Genesis 16:6). These simple words make me weep. How can a woman and man of promise treat another human being so cruelly, particularly one carrying their own child? God help them! God help Hagar! God help us!

God met Hagar in the middle of her wilderness. And God insured the care of Hagar and her son. Not only on this occasion, but also later in Genesis when Sarah again became jealous of Hagar and her son, Ishmael. Again, Sarah caused Hagar to leave, and again God provided for Hagar and her son. Even though God was clear that the promise was for Sarah and Abraham, God continued to make different promises to Hagar. Hagar, too, was a person of promise. God saw Hagar. And she "gave this name to the Lord who spoke to her: 'You are the God who sees me,' for she said, 'I have now seen the One who sees me'" (Genesis 16:13).

Never believe the lie that you are no longer part of God's promise, whether you are Hagar, Sarah, or even Abraham in your own story. God saw Hagar and God sees you! I know that God saw Jessie when a mean girl attempted to speak a limitation prophecy over her. I imagine God whispering in Jessie's ear, "Don't listen to her. She's hurting on the inside too. Jessie, you are my beloved. You are fearfully and wonderfully made!" Do you realize that when God created you, God didn't create junk? You were not a misstep or mistake. Rather, God is working desperately to help you see what God sees in you.

In this moment, Hagar was despised and mistreated, but God made her a promise and reminded her that God sees her! If you are grieving because of a great loss, God sees you. If you are in panic because of harsh words spoken over you, God sees you. If you suffer from chronic illness, God sees you! If you are surrounded by people but feel all alone, God sees you. No matter which player you are in the comparison game, God sees you.

Have you noticed that when you do something—screw up, disobey, or sin—that God is not quick to remind you of how big of a screw-up you are but is ready to remind you of your identity in God? In the very next chapter after

Sarah has mistreated Hagar, this happens: "God also said to Abraham, 'As for Sarai your wife, you are no longer to call her Sarai; her name will be Sarah. I will bless her and will surely give you a son by her. I will bless her so that she will be the mother of nations; kings of peoples will come from her'" (Genesis 17:15-16).

Sarah's disobedience did not change her identity in God. And it did not change God's promise to her. Sarah was called and claimed to be mother of nations. And it is the same with us. I am not saying that we can do whatever we want, but I am saying that nothing we do separates us from the identity that we have in God. You are a beloved son, you are a beloved daughter, of God.

Sometimes self-righteous types like me can get a little excited about stuff like this in the Bible. We think, *What do you mean God just kept the promise? That's not fair! Come on, God, Sarah did not deserve that.*

No, Sarah did not deserve God's grace. Sarah did not deserve God's love, and certainly Sarah did not deserve to be heir to God's promise. But I think she understood that God's grace was not deserved because later in the narrative, when God reaffirmed the promise to Sarah and Abraham through three strangers, Sarah was surprised:

> Trust the promise that God has placed in your life. Trust your inner fierce, because God loves you just as you are.

"So Sarah laughed to herself as she thought, 'After I am worn out and my lord is old, will I now have this pleasure?' Then the LORD said to Abraham, 'Why did Sarah laugh and say, "Will I really have a child, now that

I am old?" Is anything too hard for the Lord? I will return to you at the appointed time next year, and Sarah will have a son'" (Genesis 18:12-14).

God was not yelling at Sarah. God was not getting on her for laughing because she had a lack of faith. I believe God was saying to Sarah, "Don't you understand just how much I love you? Sarah, don't you know how chosen you really are? Don't you trust my promise to you? I'm the God of the universe! I've chosen you, Sarah, not only to be the mother of Isaac, but to be the mother of my nation, my people, the mother of my family!" Now Sarah had a choice to make: either she continued to believe the lies that everyone had been telling her—you are too old, it's not going to happen—or Sarah could trust God's promise.

And Sarah chose to trust. Sarah finally saw herself the way that God saw her: as the mother of nations. What was the result? A year later, at the ripe young age of ninety years old, Sarah was holding God's promise in her arms. Isaac was born! "Sarah said, 'God has brought me laughter, and everyone who hears about this will laugh with me.' And she added, 'Who would have said to Abraham that Sarah would nurse children? Yet I have borne him a son in his old age'" (Genesis 21:6-7). It's hard for me to imagine my reaction to my ninety-year-old great grandmother saying to the family, "I'm pregnant!" But the Bible specializes in miracles, whereas my faith merely dabbles.

You and I have a choice to make. Do you trust what God says about you? Or do you trust what others say? Several years ago, I had a group of friends that I ran with, and one day they decided I was the person to beat. I am competitive by nature, a natural achiever, and so I make it easy for people to want to beat me. Mob mentality is and was real. Soon I was cut out of group runs, support, cheering, and any other form of encouragement. I tried to pretend I wasn't affected by it. Besides, my only real competition was between "me and the clock." But they all did everything in their power to make sure I knew I wasn't liked. They were out to beat me in every race. They were cruel, catty, and just plain mean.

Sometimes bullying comes from people thinking we lack something, but sometimes jealousy creates another version of bullying. For a while, I believed what they said about me, and it affected more than my running times on the course. Too often, we forget that we are whole human beings: that discouragement in one area of our lives translates to other areas. If you want to defeat me, then make this extrovert feel isolated and alone. You will begin to destroy me from the inside out. And that's what they had begun to do. But then, whether through another running buddy or a mentor, I was reminded that I am a daughter of promise. I didn't have to listen to their lies about me. I could be all that God wanted me to be. I was fierce.

Rachel, never believe the lie that you are no longer part of God's promise! Choose trust! Choose genuine fierce!

Looking Back

What ever happened to Jessie? I really don't know. On occasion, I try to look her up on Facebook or ask mutual friends to see if I can make a connection. I've not been able to find her. I know I said I was sorry as a seventh grader, but I realize the limitation prophecy that I spoke over her life and I want to give her a new one. I want to speak life into Jessie. If I ever find her, this is what I want to say:

Jessie, you are a beautiful, beloved daughter of God. Nothing that you do or don't do can change that.

You are an exquisite masterpiece just the way you are. And sometimes, mean girls like me speak out of fear and their own broken self-image in attempts to make them feel better about themselves. It doesn't make them feel better. Please don't listen to what my seventh-grade self told you. I was wrong and cruel and should have never said the word over your life that I said. You are loved, you are bold, you are fierce!

Most of us have some kind of struggle with self-image. But no matter how many times you go under the knife, no matter how many fad diets or training programs or supplements— it will never be enough. Because you, for some reason, don't think that you're enough. You've believed the lie that you are not enough. Someone has told you something about the picture of yourself and, well, you are convinced they are right.

How does this happen? How do we get into such a dark place that we see ourselves in this way? This isn't about how others see us, and it certainly isn't about the way that God see us! But somehow, we've got this totally screwed up picture of ourselves. It doesn't have to be that way. You can be a son or daughter of God if you would just trust. Trust the promise that God has placed in your life. Trust your inner fierce, because God loves you just as you are. All you have to do is believe it.

Think about the mirror in your bathroom. What do you see when you are shaving in the morning? What do you notice when you are doing your hair? Do you smile? Are you fierce? Nope, too often when we look in the mirror, we don't smile at ourselves. Perhaps we are too focused on the color of our hair, the blemish on our face, the way our teeth look, or whether our brows are on point. But we don't smile. Why? Because we can't see ourselves the way others see us. And we certainly can't see ourselves the way God sees us. It makes me think about that little girl in her Wonder Woman costume. When I stood in front of the mirror, I twirled, spun around and around, delighted by what I saw. That little girl always smiled. At five years old, I had no fear of what I saw in the mirror, no negative thoughts, just pure joy. What happened?

As we grow up, as we play the comparison game, and as we judge ourselves and others too harshly, what happens to our self-image? What happens to our eyes that eventually makes them blind to what God sees?

Maybe we can smile at ourselves. Find a mirror and stand in front of it. Okay, this isn't some cheesy self-esteem exercise, but seriously—find a mirror. What do you see? Now you are going to be tempted to point out what you don't like—stop it. You are beloved. God loves you just the way you are. When God created you, God created a beautiful masterpiece. I am amazed by you. Do you see what other people see? You have a gift. You are courageous. I can't wait to hear your story. Do you see what God sees? Is there joy? Do you smile? Don't buy the lie that you are not enough, because you are enough!

Fierce or Force

Every day, we have a choice to make: we can use our fierce as force and harm the people around us, or we can allow a fierce rooted in love to radiate in us and through us. We can choose a life-giving fierce over force.

To my middle-school daughter: Parenting is complicated. On one hand, I don't want you to see all of the mistakes that I have made over the years. It seems easier to let you think that I am some form of perfect parent. But on the other hand, when I look back to middle school, I realize my parents' veneer of perfection was wearing off.

Someday, you will experience the full measure of my humanness. It's more important for me that you understand the power that you wield within yourself to choose: you can be kind, you can be bold, you can be smart, you can be tough, and you can be a fierce positive force. We don't have to have "Jessie experiences" in our schools and neighborhoods, and we don't have to have them in our world. I'm sorry that we adults tend to be really bad examples.

Whether in private or public, whether in church or in politics, we keep on playing the comparison game. Meanness is not a virtue. People are going to say things to you that are cruel. They will make fun of you in ways that crush you. They will point out those things that you already see as imperfections and flaws. Honey, they are not imperfections and flaws. What you see is growth. You are a work in progress. Your body, your brain, your capacity to understand all that you feel and think is expanding. That process can be awkward and painful.

Give yourself grace, and even when you want to tell yourself some lie about yourself, remember child: you are beloved. God sees you! God notices you even when you feel like you are alone. I wish that I could protect you from all pain (that's my helicopter parent talking), so I pray, "Please, sweet Jesus, make this easy for her." But it's the painful things, the hard things, the adversarial things that help us grow. Fierce is forged in the fires of adversity and challenge. There's no way to walk the path fierce without pain. You do not walk alone. I am with you, but more important, God sees you. You, my daughter, are fierce!

So What?

Has your fierce ever turned into force?

When has someone else's fierce been a source of pain for you?

Were you bullied in middle school? Were you a bully in middle school?

Is there anyone in your life to whom you would like to say, "I am sorry"?

How do you see yourself? How do you see others?

How can we work together to eliminate "Jessie experiences" in our schools, across our neighborhoods, and throughout the world?

4

FIERCE REBELLION

Now the betrayer had arranged a signal with them: "The one I kiss is the man; arrest him and lead him away under guard." Going at once to Jesus, Judas said, "Rabbi!" and kissed him. The men seized Jesus and arrested him. Then one of those standing near drew his sword and struck the servant of the high priest, cutting off his ear. "Am I leading a rebellion," said Jesus, "that you have come out with swords and clubs to capture me?"

Mark 14:44-48

Breaking Up Fights

I t was the end of the day. We had just gathered for a high school assembly in the gym, and most folks were ready to get on the bus and go home. The hallways were crowded and loud, but soon that low rumble of high school gossip and drama was overpowered by the sounds of fists hitting flesh.

I couldn't see what was happening, but an entire group of high schoolers was pulling together in the hallway to watch what was going on. Signs of shock, surprise, and a bit of entertainment covered their faces. I was walking with my boyfriend down the hall when we arrived on the scene. Even though I didn't know exactly what was going on, something within me just snapped.

I made my way through the crowd of students and found myself standing before two girls who were beating the tar out of each other. These two were throwing each other up against lockers and swinging with all their might. Their anger and violence didn't give me any chance to think. I ran in between the two, fully expecting to catch a punch to the face, and grabbed both by the shirts. I tore them apart and, in all of my seventeen-year-old glory, shouted, "Stop fighting, right now!"

I don't know who was more surprised by my actions—the girls, the students who were congregating, or me. For what seemed like an eternity, we just all stood there frozen by this strange act of insane courage. I wasn't a teacher; I didn't even know the two girls who were fighting. I just knew that whatever was going on between them wasn't worth beating each other's faces in. As we stared, the girls just stopped, looked at one another, made sure they called each other some profanity, and walked away.

When I turned around, it seemed that I had two hundred eyeballs staring back at me. What just happened? As the adrenaline left my body, I wanted to be anywhere else but in front of that group of people. By the time I made it back to my boyfriend and our friends, I was in tears. "What was that?" I said. "I don't know what just came over me." My friends responded with words of encouragement, "Rachel, that was amazing!" And, "I knew you were different, but that was unbelievable!"

My reputation grew as a person who was willing to fight, particularly for those who couldn't fight for themselves. I knew those young women had a purpose and destiny bigger than a hallway brawl, and I wanted to show them that I was willing to sacrifice a punch to the face to help them see it. "You must have some serious guardian angels," my boyfriend remarked.

That day I realized that we all have a fierce that is deep within. And when the right circumstance arises, we have a choice to make: to be the people who stay on the sidelines or the person willing to get in the fight. Hundreds of students hung back in the hallway that day, but only one had the courage to tell those girls, "You're better than this. You don't have to resolve conflict this way!" The fierce within us was planted in our heads and in our hearts by the God of the universe, pointing us to a mercy and justice bigger than ourselves.

People all over the world are getting the tar beat out of them, but too often people are too busy, too scared, or too lured by the entertainment value of it all to step into the fight. When I say *the fight*, I am not talking about social media posts, private conversations, and the justice swag you sport. I am talking about stepping up and stepping into the fight. If fierce is something that we hoard for ourselves to make us better, bigger, or more famous, well, that breed of fierce isn't fierce at all. Fierce is a gift to the human community. It's a virtue to be employed so that when people are not rightly seen, or when they refuse to rightly see others, we can fight for the right stuff together. But this brand of fierce is costly. It's going to force you to rock the boat, make waves, and cause people on all sides of the political spectrum to feel uncomfortable. If you are not making people mad across the political map, I am not sure that your brand of fierce is authentic to the human experience.

On the Way to Gethsemane

Jesus asked his followers to do what, on the surface, seemed like a strange task: go to someone's house and ask for a colt. "When they question why you are taking the colt, just tell them I need it. They will give it to you," Jesus said, and for some reason, it worked. The disciples showed up with a colt and Jesus rode it into the city of Jerusalem. In the Christian tradition, we celebrate Jesus's triumphal entry into Jerusalem with Palm Sunday. It ignites our observance and celebration of Holy Week.

> *When they brought the colt to Jesus and threw their cloaks over it, he sat on it. Many people spread their cloaks on the road, while others spread branches they had cut in the fields. Those who went ahead and those who followed shouted, "Hosanna!" "Blessed is he who comes in the name of the Lord!" "Blessed is the coming kingdom of our father David!" "Hosanna in the highest heaven!"*
>
> Mark 11:7-10

What do we hear when Jesus enters the city? Celebration! We've been conditioned to believe that Jesus was being celebrated as a king. We hear this story with religious ears. Jesus is the Savior, and Jesus is the King. But that's not exactly what the people in the first century heard. Of course we know now that they were wrong about this guy, but it wouldn't be until the end of the week that they would realize it.

It's difficult to peel back the layers of theological assumption to know why the folks in Jerusalem were celebrating. But we do know that they believed that Jesus's entry into the city was about something other than merely saving people from their sins. Somehow, in modern times, we have come to segregate portions of our lives into nice, neat categories. There is the church category, the social category, the everyday life category, and the political category. Honestly, nowadays, many of us in the church attempt to avoid the political category, but not folks in the first century. They didn't have separate categories for social life, religion, and politics—no, they were all one and the same.

Jesus was a Jew, and in those times, that had both political and religious implications. If we imagine Jesus's triumphal entry into Jerusalem with those ears and eyes, we realize that he was riding into the city as some kind of political war hero—parading through the streets as a sign of Israel's power and victory. People were thinking, *Finally, someone who will stand against the principalities and dark powers of this world,* namely, the Roman government.

Jesus is here to set us free, they thought, and not only from our sins but from those who seek to oppress and destroy the people. The participants in this first-century parade wanted Jesus to fight. The Roman occupation was crushing in on their everyday lives, and they needed someone to step in and change it. Even though the scene is familiar—this is the kind of stuff political folks do—something different was happening that day in Jerusalem. Jesus rode in not on a Roman war horse but on a donkey. This was a sign of peace and humility. Something strange was going on here. Jesus was determined to stay in Jerusalem, but not to fight a battle with swords and clubs. Even so, he was there to fight and win a victory to set the world right for all people.

Fast forward to a few days later when those shouts of celebration are a far cry in the distance. Now Jesus has gathered his disciples for their

> I have read about protests in the 1960s, but do people—faithful people—still do this kind of thing?

69

last meal together. They'd eaten together, they'd broken bread together, and Jesus had done all he could to warn them of the challenges that lay ahead. After the meal, Jesus traveled to the Mount of Olives and Gethsemane, where he was so anxious and so disturbed that you get this feeling that he might just fall apart right then and there. Jesus was deep in prayer and asked his disciples to pray, but they either didn't or couldn't or wouldn't. Instead, they struggled to stay awake. We find Jesus frustrated and disappointed. Then suddenly the story takes a turn.

> *Just as he was speaking, Judas, one of the Twelve, appeared. With him was a crowd armed with swords and clubs, sent from the chief priests, the teachers of the law, and the elders. Now the betrayer had arranged a signal with them: "The one I kiss is the man; arrest him and lead him away under guard." Going at once to Jesus, Judas said, "Rabbi!" and kissed him. The men seized Jesus and arrested him. Then one of those standing near drew his sword and struck the servant of the high priest, cutting off his ear. "Am I leading a rebellion," said Jesus, "that you have come out with swords and clubs to capture me?"*
>
> Mark 14:43-48

Getting Arrested

As a first-year seminary student, I was walking to class with a friend of mine when she turned to me and said, "Did you hear? A group of first years got arrested this weekend!" There was almost excitement in her voice.

"Arrested?" I questioned. "Why?" I couldn't imagine a group of future pastors getting themselves into that kind of trouble. "What were they doing?"

"Protesting," she said, "at a state-sponsored execution."

I couldn't believe what I was hearing. I came from a place where good Christian boys and girls kept all the rules, took pride in being polite to those in positions of authority, and never—and I mean *never*—got themselves arrested.

"What do you think the school will do about it? Will they get kicked out?"

"No," said my friend, stunned by my response. "A handful of professors were there with them."

What? Bible professors getting themselves arrested?

I knew at that point my concerns would fall on deaf ears. We quickly moved on to other subjects and, on the outside, it appeared as though I was listening, but in truth, I was immersed in an internal monologue: *What on earth? What is this? Students that get themselves arrested? Is this even a real thing? Don't these young women and men know better? Certainly, the professors should know better. I can't believe they led innocent seminary students astray. What if getting arrested affects their futures? How will they explain this to their future church boards? "Yes, Pastor so-and-so, we see here on your resume that you went to Duke Divinity School, but we also noted on your application that you were arrested. Do you care to explain?"*

My mind was swirling. I lived by the mantra "Keep your nose clean, follow the rules, and respect those in authority." In my experience of Jesus, there wasn't any room for getting arrested. I mean, I had read about protests in the 1960s, but did people—faithful people—still do this kind of thing? And besides, what kind of Jesus was this? What could possibly be worth getting into trouble for? This was a form of fierce that I wasn't sure I was ready or even willing to sign up for. But what had I signed up for?

Signing Up for a Rebellion

The disciple Judas had signed up for a rebellion. I bet that Palm Sunday parade gave Judas a lot of false hope, as in, *Finally Jesus is coming into his own. He's going to be the savior, the political messiah that we so desperately need around here.* Judas's perspective was that politics and power functioned in a particular way. In other words, "Get out your weapons, fellas, and sharpen your swords. It's going down. We are going to fight our way into Jesus's reign as king." What's shocking was that Judas's excitement was short-lived. Just a few days later, he was ready to hand Jesus over to the religious authorities—those men of religious and political power who wanted Jesus killed.

Some people believe that Judas did this not to betray Jesus but to force Jesus's hand—to kind of smoke the rebel Jesus out so that the fight could really begin. Judas was clever and shrewd, and he had a strategy formulated down to the last calculation. He was desperate for a rebellion. Judas had a pretty bad reputation, but when I think about what he was trying to do—to force Jesus's fierce—I realize that many of us subscribe to this kind of strategy. When things are not going our way, when the oppression continues, when folks on the margin keep getting beaten down, I hope faith-filled people are willing to stand up and fight. That was Judas! He didn't just want to sit on the sidelines. Judas wanted to fight.

As you gather with others in your religious institution on the weekend, do you ever wonder when we Christians are actually going to do something? Ginghamsburg Church is an unlikely, thriving United Methodist community of four thousand participants in four locations throughout the Miami

Valley near Dayton, Ohio. When Ginghamsburg Church began to grow, the tiny village of Ginghamsburg didn't even have a traffic light. But from those humble beginnings, the church has grown and flourished. I have served as a pastor there for five years. In 2018, the church's worship-design team retreated at an Episcopal retreat center in Sharonville, Ohio. Sixteen nuns live in intentional community at the center. We had the opportunity to sit down with one of the nuns, who told us her call story and why she became a nun. When we asked her to give us a word of wisdom, she began to talk about the political divide in our country. In all her many years of fighting for peace and justice in the world, she had never known such pain-filled division. With expectation in her voice, she asked, "What is the church going to do about it?"

What are we going to do about it? Are we going to add to the noise? Are faith-filled people going to sit on the sidelines? Are we going to take matters into our own hands and hearts? It's hard to know what to do. What I do know, though, is that Jesus didn't remain a passive figure in a very politically divisive time in history. Jesus did something about it; but Jesus's actions just weren't fast enough for some, who felt like they needed to hurry up the process. That's what Judas did. He wasn't willing to wait for whatever Jesus had planned. It was time to force the rebel Jesus out of hiding.

> *Now the betrayer* (notice that even the writer of the Gospel of Mark can't bear to say his name) *had arranged a signal with them: "The one I kiss is the man; arrest him and lead him away under guard." Going at once to Jesus, Judas said, "Rabbi!" and kissed him.*
> *Mark 14:44-45*

Think about the scene just hours before: Judas had been around the Last Supper table with Jesus. For a first-century Jew, gathering around the table was a sign of deep and sincere friendship. And now Judas was betraying Jesus with the ultimate sign of friendly affection: a kiss. The meaning of the Greek word for kiss here in Mark 14, *kataphileo*, is an "affectionate or repeated kiss." One gets the sense that Judas lingered at Jesus's cheek so that the temple thugs, those servants of the high priest, wouldn't grab the wrong guy. It's awkward and it's painful. The kiss started a series of events, which began when the servants of the high priest grabbed Jesus and someone recklessly chopped off one of their ears. And just when Judas believed he had ignited the fire of violent rebellion, Jesus stopped it.

Jesus stopped the violence, told them to put away their swords, and pointed Judas to a very different style of leadership—a strange way of being king. But this is not what Judas had signed up for! Jesus was supposed to fight, to kill the principalities and powers of the world—not die for them, too. Didn't Jesus know who the bad guys were here? The disciples were the good guys, and the religious elite and Romans were the bad guys! *There are good people and there are bad people, Jesus! Get with the program!*

People Are Not the Enemy

Sometimes I, too, feel like Judas. Not because I am particularly ready to fight (oh, there are days), but because I expect Jesus to know who the good guys are and who the bad guys are. I mean, *Come on, Jesus! The good guys are supposed to live to fight another day and, well, shouldn't the bad guys get what they deserve? Haven't you watched a Marvel movie lately, Jesus?*

We know how this stuff works. It's the myth of redemptive violence: that when we fight and kill our enemies, we are victorious. But when the story tells us Jesus didn't fight, that Jesus didn't take out the bad guys with one expert karate move, it leaves me wondering, *What brand of fierce did Jesus sign up for?*

One Sunday morning, I was sitting in church listening to a message. Something was said that led me down a mental tangent that had little to do with the message but a whole lot to do with my life. I had been frustrated with someone about something. And truth be told, I am motivated by anger. Anger fuels me. Although I don't think it's all bad to get angry about situations that I experience, there are times when my anger is less than justified. So, like a lawyer prepping for closing remarks, I built a solid case against this person in my mind. *Can you believe how they handled that situation? That was unacceptable! And they call themselves a leader.* Just about the time I was ready to mentally destroy the bad guy, I heard something within me say, "Rachel, that person is not the enemy. People are never the enemy."

Sounds simple, right? Except I was pretty ticked off at this person. They were frustrating me, and I felt pretty justified in my frustration. What if I wanted them to be the enemy? In my mind, my grievance against this person certainly was worth fighting for! I was in

> Come on, Jesus, didn't you come to forgive us our sins and missteps? What is all of this fierce rebellion language anyway? I am not the savior of the world and I am certainly not looking to get myself crucified.

75

a full-blown argument in my head and, again, something within whispered, "People are not the enemy." Dang it. The voice was right. When we label people bad or good, right or wrong, it's really easy for us to distance ourselves from their humanity. They become the object of our anger, something other than ourselves. Enemies are the bad guys or gals that we fight. But people are people. Paul, in his letter to the Ephesians wrote,

> *For our struggle is not against flesh and blood, but against the rulers, against the authorities, against the powers of this dark world and against the spiritual forces of evil in the heavenly realms.*
>
> *Ephesians 6:12*

It's the principalities and dark powers of this world that we fight against. It's broken systems, unjust laws, powers, governments, and yes, spiritual forces of evil and wickedness. You might say, "But, Rachel, people make laws and people create systems; doesn't that mean they, too, are the enemy?" No. If people can see their own humanity, their own belovedness, and that same belovedness in others, then they can fight for the right stuff. They can be part of Jesus's fierce rebellion.

New Pictures of Fierce

I was introduced to Oscar Romero in seminary. Oscar Romero was an archbishop in the Roman Catholic Church. He served the San Salvador community in El Salvador during a time of political corruption and violence. He preached against poverty, social injustice, assassinations, and torture. When he said yes to Jesus, well, that meant something. It meant that he had to follow the example of Jesus Christ no matter how dangerous it became.

In the movie that bears his name, there is a scene where Romero steps into a Roman Catholic Church to retrieve the host (the body of Jesus). Upon entering this holy space, Romero is met by military militia. They rough Romero up and send him out without the host, establishing their power and dominance over the people, even the people of God. It seems a little crazy to me that Romero would risk his life for something as simple as a few wafers of bread, but as I watch Romero return to the chapel, I realize there is so much more going on.

Romero is risking his life for the body of Christ. The Eucharist means something for Romero—it's not merely a wafer; this is the body. When Romero returns to the chapel with semiautomatic weapons pointed at his face, he not only gathers the host but serves it to the people and the militia. How can a person extend grace and life to the very people who are threatening his life and the lives of the people in El Salvador? I recall the words of the Eucharist liturgy: "The body of Christ broken for you, the blood of Christ shed for you." People are not the enemy.

What brand of fierce did Oscar Romero sign up for? Well, a fierce that says sometimes we have to risk our lives for our belief in the power of Jesus. Romero knew that stepping out in faith could cost him his life, and ultimately, it did: on March 24, 1980, while offering Mass in the chapel of the Hospital of Divine Providence, he was assassinated. Oscar Romero was murdered right in the hospital chapel.

This brand of fierce points to a cause bigger than ourselves. It's not about picking ourselves up by our bootstraps, achieving all we can achieve for our personal resumes, or even becoming famous. This fierce is a fierce that is willing to give one's life away for the sake of God's justice and redemption in the world.

But it's hard to know when to act. Sometimes I believe I have made faith in Jesus into something that God never intended faith in Jesus to be. At best, faith is a mental assent to some pretty solid values, and at worst, my own breed of religious crutch. I want Jesus, sure, but I want Jesus on my terms. *Jesus, you couldn't possibly expect me to do something about all the problems in the world. There's just too much injustice in the world to be fierce. Where do I even begin? How can I do anything about it? Come on, Jesus, didn't you come to forgive us our sins and missteps? What is all of this fierce rebellion language anyway? I am not the savior of the world and I am certainly not looking to get myself crucified.*

In a world of divisive politics, I pride myself in being able to hold the conversation together. I don't like to choose sides. I love helping people navigate their everyday lives. I want to be friends and not enemies! Do I keep the big questions at bay? No, but at least I don't tackle every single red-hot question every day. But then Jesus asked, "Am I leading a rebellion?" What am I supposed to do with this Jesus? I still feel like that shocked seminary student saying right out loud, "People do this? Real-life people do this? I thought protests were tales from liberal hippies, stuff they did when they were younger and not so wise. But good, nice, Jesus-loving folks don't lead marches, rebellions, or campaigns against the principalities and powers of this world!" But then there's Jesus's declaration right there in Gethsemane. And no matter how many times I want to do theological gymnastics around the question, it's there right in front of my face. Am I leading a fierce rebellion?

Of course, you aren't leading a rebellion, Jesus, are you? Oh, Jesus, you are? Your breed of nonviolent resistance is so shocking, your challenge to love your enemy who betrays you with the most intimate sign of friendship, your deep love is so spellbinding that,

Jesus, I don't even have a category for it. I thought I signed up for the Jesus who makes my life better, my attitude a little nicer, and my world a smaller place. Of course, the Jesus who died for you and me, the Jesus who does make our lives better, is the same Jesus who died for the redemption, restoration, and reconciliation of the whole world. *I'm not sure I get all of you, Jesus.*

When I think that I have Jesus all figured out, when I believe I have the full picture of what it looks like to follow Jesus and live a life of faith, Jesus moves on me. Okay, Jesus does not actually move, but I am blown away by a new picture of faith. It isn't the nice story that I learned in Sunday school class, its implications are bigger than my personal sin, and it makes this following-Jesus thing a whole lot harder. If living a life of fierce means joining Jesus's rebellion, then I have to actually live for more than my personal salvation and the salvation of the people I love—you know, those folks who look like me, live like me, shop like me, vote like me, and go to the church I go to. From the moment the question leaves Jesus's lips, I am uncomfortable and uncertain of my next move: *Will you join the fierce rebellion?*

Yet there are others who have heard and understood this message loud and clear. Folks like Oscar Romero and Martin Luther King Jr. gave their lives for it. People like Dorothy Day, Desmond Tutu, Nelson Mandela, Mother Teresa, and even folks who don't claim to be Christ followers, like Mahatma Gandhi, understood what kind of rebellion Jesus was leading.

I have watched students from Marjory Stoneman Douglas High School in Parkland, Florida—site of a deadly school shooting in 2018—decide that being fierce was joining the rebellion, a cause bigger than themselves. Students like David Hogg and Emma Gonzalez were thrust into the public sphere as they challenged adults to rise to the occasion and protect the lives of schoolchildren throughout the country. And no matter how forceful the opposition, no matter how menacing the death threats, these kids stayed the course. When asked why, Emma Gonzalez answered, "When we've had our say with the government—and maybe the adults have gotten used to saying, 'It is what it is,' but if us students have learned anything, it's that if you don't study, you will fail. And in this case, if you actively do nothing, people continually end up dead, so it's time to start doing something."[1]

It is time to start doing something. Too often we are more obsessed with the categories and the labels that surround our lifestyle than actually living a fierce life for Jesus.

I can't help but be inspired and convicted by David Hogg, Emma Gonzalez, and the entire March for our Lives movement that sprang from their experience. When teenagers are using their lives and their voices to mount an uprising because adults can't figure it out, I want to shout it from the rooftops: We can be better. We *should* be better.

Bottom-Up Rebellion

But even this doesn't surprise me. Fierce isn't top-down. No, fierce grows from the bottom up. It's grass roots, raw and organic. This is and was Jesus's brand of fierce. Jesus's fierce rebellion is bottom-up. And because it's bottom-up, the movement of God, the *spirit* of God, refused to be contained by those religious elites, or by the church structures or political bureaucracies of Jesus's day or ours!

Friends, this fierce is dangerous. Not the kind of danger that says, "Someone might hurt my feelings on Facebook," but the kind that moves beyond talking and 140-character Tweets. It's a danger that invades every area of our lives. It challenges us to live differently. Notice that I didn't say talk differently, post differently, or blog differently. Don't get me wrong—we can do a lot of good through social media. But when social media becomes the only thing we do to fight for the right stuff, it leaves us with a false sense of accomplishment. We can't merely sit behind computer screens to fight the injustice we see in our country. Words are powerful but have to be accompanied with real-life action. Jesus's revolution is lived out in the everyday movement of our lives—where we work, where we eat, and where we play. Is it about being nice? No, but it's also not about being a jerk, either. This form of rebellion doesn't sit proudly on religious high horses or proclaim a pious lifestyle devoid of love. Friends, Jesus's rebellion is grounded in love. And it's expensive.

The Cost of Fierce

After Jesus was seized by the temple thugs, the disciples fled. It's strange to me. These were the guys who had left their families, friends, careers, and homes to travel around with this street preacher and miracle man. I thought they knew what they were getting themselves into with Jesus. But when following Jesus became too fierce, they ran! "Then everyone deserted him and fled. A young man, wearing nothing but a linen garment, was following Jesus. When they seized him, he fled naked, leaving his garment behind" (Mark 14:50-52).

Why put this in here? Why point out this kind of desertion and flaw? I believe it's because the writer, perhaps Mark himself, wanted you to know just how dangerous it was—and is—to follow Jesus. He wanted to show you that these disciples were in real danger—enough danger that they were willing to flee naked rather than be arrested by the temple thugs. Their lives were on the line. Following Jesus is costly.

I'll never forget the first time I read about Clarence Jordan. It was in an assignment to read "The Interpretation of Scripture: Why Discipleship Is Required," by Stanley Hauerwas. Clarence Jordan's brand of fierce cut me to the core. He was committed to racial reconciliation in southwest Georgia in the 1940s. Clarence was a New Testament scholar and a farmer—you've got to watch those farmers—who founded a community called the Koinonia Farm. *Koinonia* is a Greek word used in the New Testament that means "community" or "fellowship." At first, the neighbors didn't mind too much, but as the civil rights movement gained momentum, people began to see the Koinonia Farm community as a threat. In the late fifties, the farm was having trouble getting its gas delivered even though it was against the law not to deliver gas in the winter. When things got bad, Clarence approached his brother Robert, later a state senator and justice of the Georgia Supreme Court, to legally represent him and Koinonia Farm.

His brother declined, citing all the things he might lose as a result. Clarence challenged him. "Do you accept Jesus Christ as your Lord and Savior?"

"I follow Jesus, Clarence—up to a point," Robert answered.

Robert admitted that he followed Jesus up to—but not onto—the cross. Clarence called him out and said he wasn't a disciple. He then challenged Robert to go to church and tell them that he wasn't a disciple.

"Well, now, if everyone who felt like I do did that, we wouldn't have a church, would we?"

"The question," Clarence said, "is 'Do you have a church?' "[2]

Do We Have a Church?

Do we have a church? Sometimes those simple everyday folks like Clarence Jordan function like modern-day prophets: Do we have a church? Do we understand the cost? Are we growing fierce from the inside out? When we see folks fighting on the margins, do we stand in the hallway or do we risk being punched in the face? I want to believe we do the latter.

Jesus followers believe that Jesus is the hope of the world, and that means something. This God-man went to the cross because he died for all people—and *all* means *all*. We believe that God, through Jesus Christ, ignited a bottom-up rebellion—a clarion call to all who are beaten up, broken down, oppressed, weary, and worried—that says, "Come, and I will give you life." This new life in Christ is a life that changes brokenness, a life that changes you, that changes me. It has the power—that's right, the real-life power—to change the world! We are part of a hope-filled rebellion!

Evil does not win. God has the power! God's love and light reign over a power-hungry world obsessed with winning at all costs. Friends, there is a new way to be human that we haven't even wrapped our minds around. Jesus calls us into the hope-filled way that we have been designed to live. God is declaring that you were made for this. You and I were designed to be a sign of his love-soaked rebellion, causing folks to scratch their heads and look at God's love in us with awe and wonder! We are dealers of a profound hope.

I imagine there are people in your life—where you work, where you live, and where you play—who are looking for profound hope. They are waiting for a Christian community that does more than merely tweet that they are Christian. A community that lives out a brand of fierce so authentic and genuine that others can't help but join in their Jesus-ignited rebellion. This brand of fierce is a compilation of a thousand daily decisions to say yes to being pulled into Jesus's kingdom, God's reign right here on earth as it is in heaven.

So, if you are ready for that kind of life, that kind of rebellion, then I wonder—what in your daily practice readies you to fight for the right stuff? Are you willing to get punched in the face for people you don't even know when you see their real pain? What's happening in your community, the country, and the world that impassions you to lead the rebellion? Read through the Gospel of Mark. When does Jesus make you uncomfortable? Is there anything about Jesus and the way that he lives his life that challenges the way that you live yours?

So What?

Make a list of the people who get on your nerves. Why do they bother you? Why are you frustrated?

Have you ever named the people who get on your nerves as enemies?

What does Jesus have to say about our enemies throughout the New Testament? Does Jesus's example of nonviolent resistance challenge you? Does it inspire you?

What did you think you signed up for when you signed up to follow Jesus?

What if you lived ready to be pulled into the rebellion? What if you didn't hold back?

$\approx$ 5 $\approx$

WHEN RELATIONSHIPS BOIL

While he was still talking with them, Rachel came with
her father's sheep, for she was a shepherd. When Jacob
saw Rachel, daughter of his uncle Laban, and Laban's
sheep, he went over and rolled the stone away from the
mouth of the well and watered his uncle's sheep. Then
Jacob kissed Rachel and began to weep aloud.

Genesis 29:9-11

I am a sucker for a great love story. Girl meets boy, girl falls in love with boy, and they live happily ever after. At first glance, the story of Jacob and Rachel has all the makings of a Hollywood romantic comedy. Two people meet, fall in love, ask for the dad's blessing, and tough luck, the answer is no. Okay, not really; it was more like, "No you may not marry my daughter until you work for her hand in marriage." Rachel's dad, Laban, was a strange person. The price of marriage for Jacob was costly. His marriage to Rachel would cost Jacob seven years of his life.

Many of us live far outside the culture of arranged marriage or marriages within family lines. Understanding a world of wedding dowries and a culture of honor and shame is a challenge for our current relationship sensibilities. But even Laban's demand seemed a little bit steep, even in his context. And yet, Jacob was not fazed by Laban's proposal. "No problem," he thought. "Rachel's worth it."

> After Jacob had stayed with him for a whole month, Laban said to him, "Just because you are a relative of mine, should you work for me for nothing? Tell me what your wages should be." Now Laban had two daughters; the name of the older was Leah, and the name of the younger was Rachel. Leah had weak eyes, but Rachel had a lovely figure and was beautiful. Jacob was in love with Rachel and said, "I'll work for you seven years in return for your younger daughter Rachel." Laban said, "It's better that I give her to you than to some other man. Stay here with me." So Jacob served seven years to get Rachel, but they seemed like only a few days to him because of his love for her.
>
> *Genesis 29:15-20*

The thought of Jacob serving Laban for seven years for Rachel's hand in marriage makes me sigh. This sacrificial form of love is inspiring. But before sentimentality clouds our vision, we need to look at the rest of the story, because the rest of the story points to the complications of marriage, family, and relationships.

Jacob did exactly what Laban asked. Wedding preparations were made, and everything seemed to be going as planned until after the wedding night. When Jacob woke up the next morning, he discovered the bride in his bed was not Rachel but her older sister Leah. Laban had some explaining to do! This seems like a cruel trick. Not only had Laban deceived Jacob, but he had lied to his own daughters and established conflict between the two women.

*When morning came, there was Leah! So Jacob said
to Laban, "What is this you have done to me? I served you
for Rachel, didn't I? Why have you deceived me?" Laban
replied, "It is not our custom here to give the younger
daughter in marriage before the older one. Finish this
daughter's bridal week; then we will give you the younger
one also, in return for another seven years of work." And
Jacob did so. He finished the week with Leah, and then
Laban gave him his daughter Rachel to be his wife.*

Genesis 29:25-28

When I read the rest of the story, it turns my stomach to think about the way these two sisters and women were pitted against each other. Their worth and value was defined by whether they were favored by their husbands and God. And what was the sign of God's favor? Whether or not the women could have children. I understand that this was a different time, operating out of a different worldview, but my heart still grieves for the relationship between the sisters, their family, and God. Just because two people share the gift of fierce does not mean their relationship isn't complicated.

I met my husband Jon in high school French class. My friends and I would make fun of him and his friends because they were such class clowns. Although Jon enjoyed making people laugh, he was also a natural leader. Sometimes his leadership challenged the people around him to make something better of themselves, and other times—well, it landed him in the office during band practice. Jon and I had flirted on a band and choir trip to Toronto, but we didn't start dating until the time we hung out at a youth gathering at the local YMCA. After I beat Jon in a few rounds of one-on-one basketball, he ended up asking me that night if I was going to the Sadie Hawkins dance hosted by our National Art Honor Society.

"Yes," I said. I could see that he was disappointed with my answer. "But I don't have a date. Do you want to go with me?" I said with cheerful anticipation.

He didn't hesitate. "Absolutely!"

And that's all she wrote. Well, sort of. There is a real gift in dating and then marrying your high school sweetheart. You have a shared history. Your school, friends, family, community, and activities were and are all the same. When you talk about the past, you don't have to explain why a joke was so funny or who the main characters were; you both just know, because you were there to experience it.

But there was pain in that shared history too. We each knew the other's relationship history, for example. Our relationship when we were teenagers wasn't always smooth sailing either. There were frustrations, fights, and breakups. I've always said that we had to grow up together, and growing up together can be really complicated. So, at the ripe old ages of twenty and twenty-one, we decided to get married. My parents were not thrilled. "Rachel, are you sure about this?" my mom questioned. "What if you don't finish college?" My mom's reservations made me all the more eager to tie the knot. Besides, we were in love. We also knew that our relationship was at a crossroads. We were serious. So, it was either stay serious or move away from each other for life.

The night before our wedding day, I remember talking with my mom and being frustrated by something that Jon had or hadn't done.

"You know, Rachel, you don't have to do this!" my mom said, giving me an out.

"Don't say that, Mom!" I erupted in tears. The truth was, I knew I didn't have to do this—I didn't have to do anything—but I wanted to marry Jon Billups. And so, we married on July 28, 2001, following my sophomore year and Jon's junior year of college.

Although I may have been a bit of a bridezilla leading up to the wedding, our wedding was a blast. We enjoyed every moment of that day. The celebration with friends and family was tangible, and many believed we had made a great decision for our future. We certainly had. But it didn't take us long to realize we didn't have all the tools we needed in our relational toolbox to have a happy and healthy marriage.

Our first year of marriage was pretty good. We got along reasonably well and tried to work out conflicts on the spot. We didn't have a lot of time to get ourselves into too much trouble. We were full-time students, Jon studying to be in Physical Education and me attempting to finish a degree in Bible and Religion. We both were college athletes. Jon played football, and I ran track and cross-country. In order to eat through the week, we had to have part-time jobs, so shortly after those "I dos," we quickly found ourselves in the world of adulting.

But when the first year bled into the second, and Jon was student teaching, I was working on an honor's thesis. Our lives went from manageable to chaotic. We became short with ourselves and bitter with one another. We both had fierce personalities. Jon and I both are natural leaders and extroverts, and we like being in charge. Our fights were more than small arguments; they were all-out relationship wars! We began questioning the decision to marry so young. I wondered if I had picked the right one. I had this spiritual naiveté that said,

"If I am a Jesus follower and my husband is a Jesus follower, marriage should be easier than this."

Jon spent his evenings hanging out with the guys, and I was too insecure to give him the room to enjoy time with his friends. The fights became more frequent and the bitterness more intense until one night, after I fixed dinner for Jon and a friend, they went back to his apartment to play video games. When I called late into the night to ask for my husband to come home, his friend answered the phone and said, "He's not coming home." When I said "I do," I didn't say "I do" to this!

We lived in an old house split into apartments. There was a large apartment on the bottom floor and two apartments on the top. The two on the top were really a series of bedrooms retrofitted into apartment spaces. The walls were paper thin. I remember praying that the person next door wouldn't call the cops or turn us in to the campus police for the screaming matches we began to have at night.

Jon and I had been attending a church in town and began developing a relationship with the youth pastor and his wife. They had been married longer than we had and were parenting a couple of kids. We knew we needed help, so we mustered up the courage to tell them we were struggling. Things didn't go as planned. Our vulnerability gave them permission to be vulnerable as well. They, too, were struggling and seemingly worse than we were. Although it was nice to know we were not alone in the struggle, the conversation did not lead us to forms of relationship health.

So Jon and I became experts in hurting one another and hiding our true pain and feelings. We each had habits and hang-ups that further damaged our marriage relationship. We dealt with our pain in individual and destructive ways:

controlling sex, flirting with other folks for attention, drinking too much, or blaming the other person for all our unhappiness. Our relationship was a mess. But we were too afraid to go to the counselors on campus. We had heard horror stories about students confessing their destructive behaviors and getting kicked out of school. We couldn't afford to get kicked out. So, we fought our way to graduation.

After graduation, we were on our way to Pilot Mountain, North Carolina. I had a pre-discernment field-study placement at First United Methodist Church through Duke Divinity School. This sleepy little town just outside of Mayberry—that's right Mount Airy, North Carolina—seemed like the perfect place for us to simmer into some healthier habits. And besides, we were living with a couple who housed us, so we would have to be on our best behavior. But when your relationship is a mess and you've spent the last year hurting and hiding, you can't pretend forever.

I remember it like it was yesterday: Jon and I found ourselves in a terrible fight. I had discovered some of his destructive habits and he mine. Hurt by each other's hiding, we took it upon ourselves to tell each other the truth about everything we had been holding back for years. When I looked at my husband, I wasn't sure who I had married, and I am sure he felt the same way. This was a crossroads. We had done enough damage to each other and to our marriage relationship that we had a choice to make: recognize we were powerless to make this marriage any better and get some help, or divorce.

"What do you want to do?" I asked, barely able to breathe.

"Rachel, I don't know what to do," Jon replied.

"We can't keep living this way. I hate this, and soon I am going to hate you."

I had never felt that kind of pain in my life before. I had lost people I had deeply loved, but to experience the kind of brokenness we were experiencing in our marriage almost seemed unbearable.

> It's easy to be objective when things aren't heated, when standing on the cool-down side of an argument, but in the moment, using the words always and never characterize family members, limit friendships, and destroy the connection between spouses.

"Rachel, when we got married, we said divorce was not an option." Jon declared. "We owe it to ourselves to try to get some help."

I still remember sitting in the car riding to Durham with Jon for a job interview and weeping. "I don't think I will recover from this," I said. "It hurts so bad, I can't breathe."

Looking back, I now recognize that I had been suffering from clinical depression for a while. Our marriage issues had merely exacerbated my already darkened mental state. I didn't feel safe telling my supervising pastor what was going on, so Jon and I traveled to Duke University in Durham, where we saw a counselor and I saw a psychiatrist.

I had reservations about seeing a counselor who wasn't a Christian counselor, but this counselor was included in my student health fee, so it was all we could afford. That decision to get some relationship tools in our toolbox changed our lives.

"You all can make this work, but you are going to have to work at it," our counselor declared. She was right. Marriage is not the wedding day; marriage is a lifetime of saying, "I choose you," to your partner every single day. The truth was, many of our relationship issues were complicated by the fact that we needed to grow up. Both Jon and I needed more relational and mental stability in our own lives so that we could be a life-giving source for another.

Perhaps the biggest truth that I discovered about myself in that season of my life was that I was waiting for Jon in order to do nearly everything I wanted to do. I wanted to be healthier and exercise, I wanted to change my eating habits, I wanted to save money, and I wanted to spend more time reading than watching TV. *But if Jon isn't doing them,* I thought, *how can I do the things I really want to do?* I can't imagine how codependent I must have seemed to my counselor. I had just thought married couples did everything together. But when my counselor opened my eyes to the reality that I couldn't control Jon and that I was merely responsible for how I thought, felt, and acted, she set me free. Jon and I worked on interdependence rather than codependence. We wanted a whole and healthy relationship where he could be Jon and I could be Rachel.

Expecting the Impossible

Although Jacob loved Rachel and favored Rachel over her older sister Leah, Leah had children and Rachel did not. This created tension in the relationship. Bitterness grew between the sisters, and family rivalry was firmly established. Each person in the story began to come to the relational table with unhealthy expectations. These were not only expectations of one another but also expectations of God. God needed to do something about this relationship mess. As I read through Genesis 29 and 30, it seems to me that both Leah and Rachel perceived Jacob's God to be a genie-in-a-bottle kind of God. They wanted God to be readily available to grant their relationship wishes. Things got so heated between Leah and Rachel that Rachel pleaded with Jacob in desperation.

> *When Rachel saw that she was not bearing Jacob any children, she became jealous of her sister. So she said to Jacob, "Give me children, or I'll die!"*
>
> *Genesis 30:1*

What kind of expectation is this? Jacob cannot magically give Rachel a child. I get that Rachel didn't understand the process of reproduction the way the we do, but the expectation on Jacob, and frankly on God, is enormous. Unhealthy expectations of our spouses can lead to the destruction of a relationship. I had some really unhealthy expectations of our marriage and of Jon. And perhaps the unhealthiest of my expectations was that I thought Jon could make me happy. As though somehow, he would complete the broken relationship puzzle in my heart and head. But no human, no person, is designed to completely satisfy all of my relational needs. It's a gruesome expectation to think that I wouldn't need friends, colleagues, family members, and real-life people to help round out my relationship appetite.

Even though it wasn't the counselor's advice, I began praying for Jon on a regular basis. I realized that I was hypercritical of his actions: "You never run with me! You always want to play video games. You never want to do what I want to do."

In every intimate relationship, there is the temptation in our frustration to speak out of our pain. And when we do, many of us employ the two most potentially destructive words in the English language, *always* and *never*. *You always bring her up! You never seem to listen! All I'm asking for is a little support but you never have time for me anymore. You always do that!*

Always and never. It's easy to be objective when things aren't heated, when standing on the cool-down side of an argument, but in the moment, using the words *always* and *never* characterize family members, limit friendships, and destroy the connection between spouses. I was limiting the potential health of our relationship because of the words I spoke over Jon. I also recognized that Jon was living into my criticisms. It was as if I were speaking a prophetic word over the future of my marriage, and the outcome was less than pleasant. I remember being convicted of using criticism and God urging me to pray for Jon. I heard, "Rachel, your complaining isn't helping. You need to pray for him."

"But God, he's not living up to his promises!" I would protest.

"Rachel, he's not going to if you keep speaking negativity into his life!"

So, I started to pray: I prayed that Jon would live into the purpose and promise God had for his life. I prayed for God's agenda for Jon's life and not mine. My prayerful words of affirmation included, "Jon, you are going to be a wonderful father, a solid friend. You will lead a new generation to discover their purpose and God's plan for their lives. I can't wait to see the man that you become."

As I began to pray these affirming words for my husband, something happened. Not only in Jon but also in me. It is really difficult to be cranky about and frustrated with a person that you are continually affirming. I realized that these prayers became part of the solution to my problem. I began to see Jon and my marriage differently. This was no longer a relationship that I was desperate to control, but rather a gift that would and could grow into a life-giving marriage.

What Is Love?

Love is patient, love is kind. It does not envy, it does not boast, it is not proud. It does not dishonor others, it is not self-seeking, it is not easily angered, it keeps no record of wrongs. Love does not delight in evil but rejoices with the truth. It always protects, always trusts, always hopes, always perseveres. Love never fails. But where there are prophecies, they will cease; where there are tongues, they will be stilled; where there is knowledge, it will pass away. For we know in part and we prophesy in part, but when completeness comes, what is in part disappears. When I was a child, I talked like a child, I thought like a child, I reasoned like a child. When I became a man, I put the ways of childhood behind me. For now we see only a reflection as in a mirror; then we shall see face to face. Now I know in part; then I shall know fully, even as I am fully known. And now these three remain: faith, hope and love. But the greatest of these is love.

1 Corinthians 13:4-13

Although I don't want to be hypercritical of Jacob, Rachel, and Leah, their form of fierce love seems dysfunctional at best. For starters, we no longer affirm the social position that these women found themselves in. Although you can watch television specials on people who practice polygamy, there is a reason it's not our social norm. Within the context of Christian marriage, a couple's love is to be a glimpse of Jesus' love for the church. If you read through most traditional marriage liturgies, you recognize that the entire ceremony is centered around the image of Jesus' sacrificial love for the church, the body of Christ, as the model for marriage. It's the reason, when we come to "giving and receiving of rings" part of a marriage ceremony, that I remind the couple of the vows they are getting ready to make.

"Do you see this ring? It's a perfect circle. It has no beginning and no end. It reminds us of God's love," I begin. The rest goes something like this:

> God's love has no beginning and no end. It's not conditional. We, as human begins, have limited love. Most of the time, we love the people around us when we feel like it. I love you until you do something that jeopardizes that love. But not God's love. God loves you period. Our love for our spouse gets frustrated, cranky, and irritable. When you are having one of those moments in your marriage relationship when you are so annoyed with your spouse, I want you to look down at your wedding ring and be reminded of God's love. You see, you can't love your spouse with your limited love. You need God's love. Ask God to help you love and see your spouse the way God loves and sees that person.

We love with a limited love. But God is not limited by our quirks, our hang-ups, or the baggage we bring into a marriage relationship. God is not limited by our limited love.

Jon and I recognized the fierce within each of us. We wanted to live a full and courageous life. We wanted to have a fierce marriage. But the only way that was going to happen was for each of us to affirm one another's gifts and to continually, with honesty and vulnerability, expose each other's hang-ups.

Jon and I have found ourselves teaching the Alpha Marriage course at Ginghamsburg Church. We are not marriage experts, but we believe it's important to share our story with people so that they, too, can have the courage to journey toward a fierce marriage relationship. And with each new class, Jon and I learn a lot about our own marriage relationship. Our favorite part of the class is the homework.

We've made it a regular practice in our marriage relationship to spend time with each other. As parents of young children, we have found this to be increasingly difficult. We began with making sure our kids were in bed early—like 7 p.m. early. Putting our kids to bed early insured Jon and I time to talk, plan, and enjoy each other's presence. But even that didn't seem intentional enough, so we began to plan regular overnight getaways. Sometimes it was as simple as eating dinner out and staying at a hotel just a few miles away while the grandparents watched our kids. Other intentional dates included going to see our favorite band, a trip to Chicago, eating at the home of a local chef, or retreating with other couples. As we have added to our family, finding such time away has been increasingly difficult. But because our kids are spread out in age, and our oldest is a teenager, many times we put the kids to bed, put the oldest in charge, and then go to a local restaurant for a drink and an appetizer. We have the reputation in the neighborhood of being the tough parents who make our kids go to bed early, but they need their sleep, and we need intentional time together.

But it's not enough just for us to spend time together. Intimacy and deep trust have to be cultivated. There are still times in my life when insecurity rears its ugly head or when we get so busy with what we need to do that we don't really see each other's relational needs. Homework from the marriage course gifts us with the opportunity to talk about our marriage in ways that we wouldn't normally, to get below the surface of our tiffs and arguments to uncover what's really happening in our heads and hearts. This practice of vulnerability doesn't always come naturally. When some of the homework questions make us uncomfortable, we have a choice to make: to go back to the practice of hiding or to healthfully navigate our brokenness and pain together. We have to choose to let each other see what is deep within our hearts and heads.

A Big Hang-Up

I struggle with my birthday. I am a December baby, and I always say that Jesus's birthday trumps mine every year. It's not really Jesus's fault. It's the season. When you are born on December 19, it's just way too convenient for people to hand you a present and say, "Happy Birthday and Merry Christmas." Couple this tendency with being the middle child, and you've got a life of hurt on your hands. I jokingly tell the story of the three birthday parties I remember my parents throwing for me. One in the first grade, one in the sixth grade, and then one more when I turned twenty-five. I was thankful for a birthday celebration at twenty-five—it was a surprise—but nothing says, "This is *only kind of* your day" like candles on my mom's half-eaten birthday cake from the week before.

99

I've got birthday issues. And through the years, birthdays have been probably one of the biggest struggles in our marriage relationship. Jon and I decided early on in our marriage that we were not going to buy each other gifts for holidays or birthdays. We planned on having lots of kids and realized it could get really pricey. So instead, we would focus on intentionally building our relationship through the year. That's what we said, but every year when it came to my birthday, I was disappointed. Not because I didn't have gifts. I didn't want gifts; I wanted someone to acknowledge my birthday. Early in our marriage the conversation around my birthday went something like this:

"What do you want to do for your birthday?" Jon would ask me.

"Oh, I don't really need anything. I just want to do something special. Surprise me," I would say. But when the surprise did not meet my birthday expectations, at best I would be disappointed and at worst I would flat-out cry. It was as if I expected Jon to pay off a birthday debt that was growing larger every year.

One year, my frustrations were so high that I was ready to spend the day alone without any interaction with Jon or the kids. It was in that place of hurt and pain that I realized I was carrying some baggage into our relationship that Jon didn't create and didn't deserve to carry. Suddenly, I realized that I had an unrealistic and unhealthy expectation that Jon was never going to fulfill. It wasn't his relationship gift. Jon was a planner, but he wasn't going to come up with the romantic evening of my dreams. What he needed from me was an idea, and what I needed from him was intentionality.

So, we compromised. We would talk about ideas for celebrating birthdays together and plan around our ever-intensifying schedule. I wouldn't just give Jon one idea; I would give him several. That way, I would be surprised but not disappointed. This became our relational approach for everything: holidays, date nights, birthdays, and future dreams. We have had some of the most life-giving marriage experiences because we have been willing to share our hopes, dreams, and expectations with each other. And we give each other permission to say, "I can't make that happen. You are expecting too much of me and my time."

I am writing this chapter on our seventeenth wedding anniversary. We've come pretty far, baby, but we have a long way to go. Like Rachel and Jacob, we, too, have relationship baggage to work through. Some of it comes from our families of origin, and some of it is from the hurt and pain we have caused ourselves and each other. We are a relationship work-in-progress. And it may sound terribly strange, but I think we are finally growing up. Time isn't the only factor to growing in relationship with each other. If that were the case, every person who was more seasoned would have a life-giving marriage relationship. But one of the reasons that our relationship is growing fiercely intimate is because we are growing ourselves. We have come to set our own personal goals for physical, mental, and spiritual health. Jon cannot supply all that I need, and I cannot supply all that he needs. We see our individual growth as an opportunity to encourage each other to become the humans God intended us to become, both as individuals and as a married couple.

In the Gospel of Mark, a religious scholar asked Jesus what was the greatest commandment. Jesus replied,

> *"'Love the Lord your God with all your heart and*
> *with all your soul and with all your mind and with all*
> *your strength.' The second is this: 'Love your neighbor as*
> *yourself.' There is no commandment greater than these."*
>
> *Mark 12:29-31*

Love God, love others, and love yourself. The commandment is not to love yourself more than others or to neglect the love of yourself for the love of others, but rather to love yourself as you love others. Through the years, Jon and I have discovered that our pictures of ourselves positively or negatively affect our relationships. If we don't love ourselves, we struggle to love one another. We struggle to embrace that fact that God made human beings to "be their true selves, their child-of-God selves" (John 1:12 MSG).

Stories Forged in Fierce

> *Then they moved on from Bethel. While they were*
> *still some distance from Ephrath, Rachel began to*
> *give birth and had great difficulty. And as she was*
> *having great difficulty in childbirth, the midwife said*
> *to her, "Don't despair, for you have another son." As she*
> *breathed her last—for she was dying—she named her*
> *son Ben-Oni. But his father named him Benjamin. So*
> *Rachel died and was buried on the way to Ephrath (that*
> *is, Bethlehem).*
>
> *Genesis 35:16-19*

The one thing that Rachel wanted the most was to compete with her sister's ability to give birth to children. And it's the one thing that killed her. It sounds strange to say, but I love these kinds of stories in the Bible. These are the real-life experiences of humans. The Bible does not edit out the drama, the pain, or the suffering of its people.

When I read about the end of Rachel's life, deep sorrow grabs my heart. Families are complicated, marriage is hard, and little in our human experience can really be characterized as having a fairytale ending. I think that's why it's so important to be authentic about the continual struggle of marriage relationships. Not everyone has a Jacob-and-Rachel experience, and not every marriage mirrors that of Jon's and mine, but we all have our issues. We all bring real baggage and pain into our relationships. It's the work of each married couple to grow into the full-life human being that God has called each of us to become.

> Fierce is more than one decision in any relationship. It's a series of saying yes to courage: the courage to tell the truth, the courage to be vulnerable, and the courage to get the help you need when you need it.

Answer to Prayer

Sometimes it takes years to recognize that God has answered your prayers. My kids and I were sitting in the worship center at church, preparing to participate in a family worship experience. Soon Jon came bounding on stage, and with a larger-than-life personality, he declared, "I am Reginald Fastidious III!" Jon loves working with children. He currently works at an elementary school as a physical education teacher with second-through sixth-grade students. "I am a rock star at my school! Everyone loves the gym teacher," Jon declares. And they do.

Although I love my children, and children in general, kids' ministry is not my gift. Jon and I, over the years, have given each other space to thrive in our own gifts, to have our own hobbies, and to be fierce in our own ways. Don't get me wrong, there are several things that we enjoy doing together: traveling, watching TV shows, playing board games, talking, trying new food, hanging out with friends, and meeting new people. I could go on for a really long time about how many things we enjoy doing together. But we are our own people. I run to stay in shape, and Jon likes to play basketball. I am a morning person, and Jon is not. I love achieving and struggle to rest; Jon makes sure that there is an even pace to his day and isn't too overly worried about his to-do list. We are different; we are married; we are fierce.

Fierce is more than one decision in any relationship. It's a series of saying yes to courage: the courage to tell the truth, the courage to be vulnerable, and the courage to get the help you need when you need it. Jon and I have not had the perfect marriage, but through all of our stumbling, we have stumbled together. We want and are willing to work toward fierce. Over the years, we have become each other's biggest fans. We are partnered together in this life. We see each other's gifts, we know each other's weaknesses, and we have a compassion for each other that comes through loving each other with God's love. With all of our marriage victory, we still recognize we are a work in progress. I believe there is a level of fierce intimacy that God wants us to discover. We aren't there yet, but I believe we have the courage to get there. We want to be fully fierce!

Marriage relationships can be a source of life and joy or even death and pain. If you are struggling in your marriage relationship or have even experienced the painful loss of marriage through divorce, I want you to know that God sees you. And sometimes the differences and choices that people make in marriage relationships do not leave room for reconciliation. But I also believe that God is a God of resurrection, and when two people are willing to work hard toward reconciliation, marriage resurrection can happen.

So What?

When you think about your most significant relationship, what unrealistic expectations do you bring to the relationship table? Does your spouse have expectations that you cannot fulfill? How are you tending to your own physical, mental, and spiritual health?

What regular practices give you time to develop your marriage relationship? Are you dating your spouse?

What season of marriage are you in? What challenges does your season of life bring to the marriage relationship?

Do you have subjects in your marriage relationship that are off limits? What makes them difficult to talk about? What would it take for you to develop a safe space for challenging conversations?

6

DEFINING MOMENTS

*You will conceive and give birth to a son, and you are to
call him Jesus. He will be great and will be called the
Son of the Most High. The Lord God will give him the
throne of his father David, and he will reign over Jacob's
descendants forever; his kingdom will never end.*

Luke 1:31-33

T hat is one heck of an announcement. Can you imagine
hanging out in your bedroom as a teenager when
suddenly this Divine Messenger shows up and lands that news
on you? When I was a teen, I freaked out when my mom came
into my room unannounced, but this kind of thing would be
crazy. Terrified—that's what I would have been. Scared out
of my mind to see a messenger of God. Teenage girl meets
"God-ordained future" sounds great, right? It sounds really
good, all except for the fact that no one in Mary's first-century
community would believe her.

Sometimes Mary doesn't seem real to me, not because of
what I read about her in the Bible but because of what I have
experienced about her through tradition. She seems holy. I can
remember at the birth of my first son, praying through the

107

night, "Hail Mary, full of grace, the Lord is with thee. Blessed are thou among women and blessed is the fruit of thy womb Jesus. Holy Mary, Mother of God, pray for us sinners now and at the hour of our death, amen." Although I am not Catholic, the labor pains of ten-pound-two-ounce Christopher Michael Billups felt like death. I needed help; I needed Mary.

Mary is to be honored, loved, and for some, even venerated. But here in Luke 1, she was scared, fragile, vulnerable, and human. Human—just the way I like my Bible characters to be. Give me humans, flaws, imperfections, and all. That's what I want to see in the Bible, because it's real, it's relatable, and it makes me realize God used regular folks to do some really amazing things. Sometimes this story gets so hijacked by Christmas that the rawness, the scandal, and its ability to be in your face nearly disappears. Life is not whitewashed porcelain nativity scenes; it's giving birth to the savior of the world in the back alley of your political oppressors. The real-life Mary was fierce.

It's easy to seem fierce, particularly when the parts of my life that people see is what I post on Instagram or Facebook. I can filter out every fear, struggle, insecurity, worry, and "I am not enough." Oh, yes, friends I have a filter for that! And that kind of in-your-face, get-out-of-my-way fierce fuels me: I think I can out-exercise, out-plan, out-calendar, out-strategize, out-cook, out-eat, out-sleep, and out-host the best of them.

But beneath the surface of that fierce is a fierce that looks at it all—not just the highlight reel, the perfect stats, or even the days that I am on my *A*-game—and says, "Rachel, we need to do something about this fear." The fears in my head and deep within my heart squeeze out the possibilities for fierce. Fierce won't force its way in. No fierce has to be fostered in the face of fear and suffering. Fierce is developed when you are face to face with those fears and insecurities. It's there that you come to a place of knowing, a place of understanding yourself and the people around you. It's deep fierce.

I was lying on an air mattress with my ten-month-old daughter, Adeline. My parents had decided to take a trip to North Carolina to visit us. They couldn't stand being nearly eight hours away from their first granddaughter, and I was delighted they were with us. Attempting to finish up seminary with a ten-month-old had come with its own challenges, and the stress of my final semester was soon upon me. Addie was giggling and bouncing on the mattress when I noticed a call coming in from my mother-in-law, Betty. They were supposed to be leaving that day to move to North Carolina for a job opportunity for my father-in-law, Steve.

The decision to move had been really difficult for my in-laws. They loved where they lived, in the heart of Hocking County, located on the edge of Appalachia. Most of Steve's family lived in that area. Betty's church, her friends, and nearly all of the relationships they had crafted in their adult lives were within twenty minutes of their home in Laurelville, Ohio. And now they were moving to Raleigh. Raleigh was nice, but it wasn't Laurelville. Although they would be within an hour's drive of Jon and me, we had already decided to move back to Ohio after seminary, and we weren't changing our minds. If they came to Raleigh, it had to be their decision—not ours. Steve and Betty decided to move. They liked Raleigh, and those mild Raleigh winters sure do look good when you're used to Ohio's subzero windchill. Steve would have a good job in the Research Triangle, and besides, his youngest brother, David, lived in Wilson, North Carolina, less than an hour away.

"Hi, Betty, how's it going?" I asked.

She was hesitating. She sounded somber and like she had been crying.

"Are you okay?" I asked.

"No," she said. "It's your Uncle David. He's, well, he's . . . Rachel, he's dead."

I have quite a few uncles on both sides of my family: my mom's brother, my dad's first cousin (who I call uncle), Betty's brother, her brother-in-law, and Steve's youngest brother. In my mind, the only possible candidate could be Betty's brother. He was older than Betty and had had some health scares, so I said, "Are you going to Arkansas?"

"Arkansas?" she replied with confusion in her voice.

"No, Rachel, not Uncle Dave, not my brother, but Steve's brother David." I nearly dropped the phone. That David was thirty-six years old. That David had a three-year-old daughter. That David was close to Jon and me, and now Betty was telling me that David was dead.

I had "met" David long before I actually met David. He was a legend. According to family accounts, David Billups was the kind of teenager every kid wanted to be: he was popular and athletic, had a great sense of humor, and pretty much did no wrong. The plot of these "David stories" was always the same: David does something that no teenager in their right mind would do, he pulls it off, he defies punishment with humor and a great smile, and everyone loves David. The End.

By the time I actually met real-life David, he had grown up. It was hard for me to equate this grown-up version to the teenage legend I had heard about, but this David had met Jesus and a wife. She was a southern belle from Wilson, North Carolina, and her accent was as big as her smile. The church had brought them together, but humor made them inseparable. They were hilarious! Always telling jokes and cutting up. They were contagious to be around. David was the youngest of the Billups brothers and about ten years older than my husband. When Jon and I married just a few years after David and his wife, we wanted to be like them. We admired their relationship, their faith, and the way they lived their lives.

Uncle David was one of my biggest fans. He took pride in knowing that Jon and I were coming to North Carolina and that his niece-in-law was attending Duke Divinity School. They bled Duke blue. Every time I visited Uncle David, he had a story about how he had told some Duke fan at work or church, "Hey, my niece goes to Duke. She's a Blue Devil!" Once we moved to North Carolina, we regularly visited them, sometimes furiously navigating the I-40 traffic on a Friday night through Raleigh just to get there.

I will never forget sitting in traffic for two hours only to arrive really late to a birthday party. We came thinking that the party was for their daughter. We even stopped by a local Walmart to buy her a present. But when we arrived, we discovered that the party was for our aunt. You should have seen her face when she opened up the present to discover a Precious Memories doll praying a good night prayer. We were mortified, but our aunt and uncle thought it was hilarious! Their special breed of laughter made any social tension dissipate.

And then there was their daughter. David loved his girl, and she loved David. Even when the relationship between Uncle David and his wife became strained, there was no doubt in anyone's mind that David was an incredible father. Their daughter was only three years old when her daddy died. David's death was complicated: separated from his wife, distant from the church, and smack-dab in a season of life that seemed to me like "delightful rebellion." It was messy. It just didn't seem like the right time!

When I finished the conversation with Betty, I ran out to the back porch, looked up in the sky, and asked God, "How much? How much suffering can one family handle?" Between us, Jon and I had lost eight close family members in two years. Some of this was the result of having had living great-grandparents, but other deaths had been just plain tragic. David's was tragic. My heart clenched. *This can't be happening! God, this seems too cruel and twisted to be real—like total human nonsense.*

> Although I have markers in my life that attempt to remind me of God's call and claim on my life, most of the time, I am wrestling between "Yes, this is it!" and "God, are you sure?"

I didn't know what else to do but to give God a piece of my mind. "Come on, God! The main reason Betty and Steve moved here was to be close to David, and now he's dead. What kind of sick cosmic joke is this? I thought you were the God of the universe. Why didn't you intervene? Why didn't you step in? Where's our *Reader's Digest* miracle? Where was David's close call? Couldn't there be a different ending than this? God, where were you? God, where are you?" I happen to believe God's big enough to handle all of my anger and smack talk. It's deep within my heart anyway; I might as well get it out. That's the point of confession, isn't it? To give words to the deep anger, fear, and sin within our hearts? I wanted God to clearly know what was in there.

Soon a call came from Grandma Barb, David's mom. "Rachel," she said, "the family would like for you do the funeral." We needed hope. They needed hope. That's what most folks are looking for at a funeral. Hope that this isn't all there is, hope that they are going to make it through this somehow, hope that some divine being is present "even in the valley of the shadow of death." That's what Grandma was asking me to do: give our family a little hope.

"Whatever you want, Grandma," I said. Although I had been asked to speak at funerals on behalf of the family on a number of occasions, I had never been expected to preside over a family funeral. And besides, I had never done a funeral in my life. And Uncle David had attended a Pentecostal church that wasn't exactly known for its openness to female ministers or seminary students. I wasn't even official! But somehow, the family talked this large church into allowing me to preside over the entire funeral, graveside and all.

I was nervous, but I wanted to honor David. I spent time contacting family and friends. Collecting stories and Scriptures and crafting a eulogy hand-drawn for David. When I arrived at the church, the pastor introduced himself. I had attended his church before, but this time was different. In this moment, we were colleagues. The pastor did his best to put me at ease and welcome me into the church. His welcome was refreshing. I have to admit, I didn't expect it, but it was there. As the celebration of David's life began, I felt a knot welling up in my throat. *Keep it together, Rachel,* I said to myself. It's not that I expected to be emotionless; I just needed to have reasonable control over my emotions.

You can't lose it all and make it through an entire funeral liturgy.

The time came for me to speak. I began with Scripture.

> *Where can I go from your Spirit? Where can I flee from your presence? If I go up to the heavens, you are there; if I make my bed in the depths, you are there. If I rise on the wings of the dawn, if I settle on the far side of the sea, even there your hand will guide me, your right hand will hold me fast. If I say, "Surely the darkness will hide me and the light become night around me," even the darkness will not be dark to you; the night will shine like the day, for darkness is as light to you.*
>
> Psalm 139:7-12

The message was clear. No matter what our circumstance, no matter how hard David had run from God, God never left David! God is with David. God is with us! When I had finished the Psalm, I said, "This is the Word of God, for the people of God, thanks be to God." A room full of blank stares glared back at me. I guess this room full of Pentecostals wasn't familiar with that piece of liturgy. And for a brief moment, I panicked. *I don't belong here*, I said to myself. But as the final words of liturgy rolled off the tip of my tongue, I heard a voice within say, *This is it. Rachel, this is what I have created you to do.*

It's not every day that a twenty-five-year-old hears a divine confirmation of purpose. And I certainly didn't expect it to happen at a funeral service. But in that moment, something holy, something other, came over me. All the anxiety, fear, and dread went out of my body, and in its stead came an overwhelming confidence and peace. *This is it! But right here, right now? In the middle of all of this pain and mess? Really, God, this moment is the moment?* You might think that as a seminary student ready to complete my final semester of divinity school, I would have already known what I was going to do, but I didn't. I still wavered. Anyone who tells you it's really easy to know your purpose is a liar. Wavering, wondering—fits and spurts of confirmation—that's my experience of call.

Although I have markers in my life that attempt to remind me of God's call and claim on my life, most of the time, I am wrestling between "Yes, this is it!" and "God, are you sure?" It seems ironic that the moment that defined who I was created to be was a moment filled with death, fear, tragedy, and mess. It certainly didn't fit a sanitized, comfortable, Christian confirmation of call, but maybe that's because I don't fit the profile of a sanitized, comfortable Christian. I am a mess—a doubting, wondering mess.

Wondering and Fear

Have you ever let fear keep you from doing something you knew you should do? Maybe a boss asked you to work on a project outside your department, or an opportunity to consider moving up to the varsity staff presented itself, or a request came in to further your education, or a move changed everything about your current life situation. Whenever I get asked to do something I've never done before, my initial reaction is usually excitement. *This could be great!* But soon, that excitement is followed by a heavy dose of fear. What if I can't do it? What if I fail? What if I am a total train wreck? What if it's not good, or what if it's not the best that someone has ever experienced? What if? Fear has been my constant companion. It's not that I think all fear is bad, but sometimes fear keeps me from doing the next right thing to step into my purpose. When fear arrives in my mind, it quickly puts a strangle-hold on the possibilities, until I find myself in purpose paralysis.

During this season of constant funerals, I was also asked to speak at Goodson Chapel at Duke Divinity School. Students were asked on occasion to speak at chapel service; it was a privilege and an honor. I was asked twice, and twice I said no. Each time, the chaplain was surprised by my reaction.

"Are you sure you don't want to do this?" she said. "You've been recommended to speak."

"Well, you see . . ." I would say, and then come up with a justifiable excuse as to why I couldn't possibly speak. "My uncle just died and I just don't have the emotional bandwidth to make it happen. I am honored, but I can't at this time."

You might think that my response was a good example of self-care. Maybe the first time it was, but I didn't have to dig deep beneath the surface of my no to find fear. I was afraid. I couldn't preach in front of all of those experts, PhDs, and world-renowned theologians. For God's sake, I was a would-be pastor, a spiritual poser at best. *How could I possibly say anything meaningful to my fellow students?* I thought. If I preached at chapel, they would find out. They would discover that I wasn't the real deal. Called, sure, but not nearly as called as the people around me. All of this is and was a self-justified form of fear. One of those no answers could have been a yes, but I was too afraid to say it.

When perfection becomes our preoccupation, we limit our lives and the lives of those around us. When fear rules the decision of the day, its creates a mental rut in our minds. It quickly becomes a pattern of response. When life is hard, when the decision is uncomfortable, when the ask seems too much,

I let fear be the first response. It becomes second nature to tell that person, that challenge, that opportunity, no.

For years I told myself that I was not operating out of fear. I was operating out of self-preservation, healthy boundaries, and a solid understanding of who I am: *That's not me, that's not what I have been created to do, I couldn't possibility do that!* But fear is dangerous when it convinces you that you are less than what you've been created to be. I spent years of my life living beneath the shade of fear and believing that any form of stepping out was contrary to my call. It's as if I said to myself, *Don't puff yourself up, don't live big, and certainly don't allow others to see all of you, because if they see all of you, well, it might be too much.* Fear kept me in my place: *If I can't win, if it isn't perfect, then I cannot do it. Rachel, stay in your box, this is your lane, don't you dare think about coloring outside of these lines!* Fear, fear, and more fear.

When people think about disobeying, most of the time they think about breaking the rules. As if God wants you and me to perpetually keep our noses clean. I don't think that's the point—the point of religion, yes, but not the point that God was trying to make with the birth of Jesus. Jesus brought new life and, with it, new possibilities for living. No, the most damaging disobedience is when you and I refuse to live fully alive. When we choose to shrink down and live small and stay within the confines of our own fears, we lose! And the world loses the chance to see our true selves, our child-of-God selves. Marianne Williamson said it this way:

> Our deepest fear is not that we are inadequate. Our deepest fear is that we are powerful beyond measure. It is our light, not our darkness that most frightens us.

We ask ourselves, "Who am I to be brilliant, gorgeous, talented, fabulous?" Actually, who are you not to be? You are a child of God. Your playing small does not serve the world. There is nothing enlightened about shrinking so that other people won't feel insecure around you. We are all meant to shine, as children do. We were born to make manifest the glory of God that is within us. It's not just in some of us; it's in everyone. And as we let our own light shine, we unconsciously give other people permission to do the same. As we are liberated from our own fear, our presence automatically liberates others.[1]

I was afraid to be fierce with every fiber of my being!

I wish I could be more like Mary: one announcement, and I am in it for life. But that's not how it works with me. Finding meaning and purpose in my life and the lives of the people around me has always been a struggle. That's why I admire Mary. This young girl, after having a divine encounter, had enough courage to ask a question, and perhaps *the* question: "How?" "How will this be," Mary asked the angel, "since I am a virgin?" (Luke 1:34). Translation: "I've been faithful to God and to the law. Unless you have some kind of magic trick up your sleeve, this isn't going to happen, God! I may be young, but I know how this stuff works. I've not done the deed."

I applaud Mary. Church types struggle to talk about bodies, sex, and sexuality, but not Mary. She understood that God had a purpose for her and that this purpose was embodied. It wasn't just a title; God was asking for all of her. When God calls each of us into our divine purpose, God calls our whole selves and our whole bodies. God is not fearful or limited by the bodies we offer to our life's purpose. Think about the excuses we give: "But, God, I am a woman." I think God's aware! "But, God, I have physical limits." "But, God, I don't look like your typical [fill in the blank]." Yep. God is not limited by the limitations we place on our bodies or on the bodies of others. All are able-bodied for God!

God decided that a teenage girl from Nazareth would be the source of life for the God of the universe, and she was. God defined all reproductive limitations to "become flesh and blood and move into our neighborhood." But when Mary asked how, God told her. "The Holy Spirit will come on you, and the power of the Most High will overshadow you. So the holy one to be born will be called the Son of God" (Luke 1:35). It's the story, our story, of creation all over again. Back in Genesis, God hovered over what was then formless and void and *ex nihilo*. Out of nothing, God created. In the Gospels, God hovered over Mary, and God once again created. This was bigger than Mary, and yet God chose Mary to bring forth new life possibilities for us all. "Mary, this is how! In the same way that I created the universe, I will hover over you and become a part of you."

If I think too hard about it, I want to weep. The redemption and healing of all of creation comes through the body of a woman. This sacred and beautiful God-act is pregnant with hope! Mary has a choice: say yes to fear or say yes to God. God was not and is not looking for perfection. God's

> When I take a thirty-thousand-foot view of my life, I think, God you've taken my mess and turned it into a beautiful miracle.

just looking for a yes. God made Mary promises, not guarantees. There was no guarantee that this journey, this purpose, this calling was going to be easy. Mary never signed up for easy. She signed up to be the very mother of God. Mary said yes. " 'I am the Lord's servant,' Mary answered. 'May your word to me be fulfilled' " (Luke 1:38).

Seventeenth Chance

I need more than one opportunity to say yes to God. For me, it's not just about second chances. I need like seventeen. I need opportunities to grow into big "yeses." I need space to fill in the well-worn ruts of fear. Deep fierce has to be built up. No matter how bold your innate personality, this type of fierce takes disciplined crafting. Because the more challenging the opportunity for life-giving purpose, the greater dose of fear.

Nearly seven years after I graduated seminary, I received a call from a mentor of mine, Pastor Mike Slaughter. At the time, Mike was the senior pastor of Ginghamsburg Church in Tipp City, Ohio. I couldn't believe it: this was the largest United Methodist Church in the state of Ohio, and he was asking me to come and preach on Mother's Day weekend. For those of you who don't know, Mother's Day is an unofficial holy day in the life of the church. There is Christmas, Easter, and then Mother's Day.

"Rachel, I need a woman to speak on Mother's Day weekend. And I think you are the right woman!" Mike said. I had some really good excuses. I was pregnant with my third child and the lead pastor of Shiloh United Methodist Church in Cincinnati, Ohio. My own church family would love for their very pregnant preacher to give a great Mother's Day sermon at her own church. And besides, it was Mother's Day, and I wanted to be with my own kids. Armed with a long list of excuses, I took a deep breath and said, "I will pray about it and quickly get back with you." Friends, that's just a nice Christian way of saying, "It's probably a no."

I was excited by the possibility, but after I got off the phone, the familiar fears began to rear their ugly heads, and the limitation prophecies I speak over my life began to play: "You couldn't possibly! Who do you think you are? Rachel, stay in your lane." I had great excuses, and it would have been a lot simpler to stay at home, preach to my own people, and say no to this opportunity. But this time, I realized that the fear was signaling something bigger in my life. Something within me said, "Rachel, this is another chance. How many times am I going to give you opportunity to grow into your full purpose and watch you turn it down?" Oh, this was *that* fear—that Duke Chapel fear. God was giving me my seventeenth chance. I made a few phone calls, made sure I had the right preacher for the weekend at Shiloh, and then I called Pastor Mike. I made sure that Mike knew all of the reasons I should say no and all the reasons I was saying yes. "Mike, I believe this is something that God is asking me to do. I've got some fears I need to overcome," I said.

Preaching at Ginghamsburg was outside my comfort zone, beyond my experience, and certainly something I could have easily run away from. I had never preached at a megachurch before. And I certainly hadn't been a guest preacher when nearly thirty weeks pregnant. But I didn't want fear to rule the day. I said yes. "I am the Lord's servant," Mary answered. "May your word to me be fulfilled" (Luke 1:38).

I would love to tell you that this yes eradicated all fear, and that from the moment of confirmation, I was filled with nothing but pure confidence. But that didn't happen. No, I said something to God like, "Okay, God, I am saying yes, and if I fail, at least I will know that I am not capable of this level of leadership." My entire family traveled to Ginghamsburg on Mother's Day weekend. If I was saying yes, we were saying yes as a family. Jon, Adeline, Christopher, and I walked into the church, and we had a sense that we might just be stepping into our future. I couldn't have been more nervous, pregnant belly, high heels, and all. But before I even stepped onto the platform, I asked God, "Help me see what you see in me." It was an honest prayer, full of fear, yes, but pregnant with possibility.

When I stepped onto that platform and saw those hundreds of faces smiling back at me, I nearly passed out. "You thought this was a good idea? Why on earth did I say yes?" With every fiber of my being, I wanted to run. But as soon as I started speaking, I heard a voice within say, "Remember, Rachel, this is what I created you to do." My body relaxed, peace came over me, and suddenly I was filled with joy. It was another confirmation of my purpose.

The weekend was incredible. There was so much positive feedback on social media that a new fear rose within me: I didn't want my church to think that I was leaving them. So, I asked not to be tagged in the social media posts. I realized that fierce wasn't some kind of feeling that I needed to muster up just to get me through the weekend. Rather, fierce was a Spirit-filled force that poured over me when I let go of fear and stepped into my purpose. Fierce had been available to me the whole time, my whole life. It's just that I hadn't given it any room in my head or my heart. I gave fear all the room it needed, without realizing fierce needed room too! Driving home that day, I said to my husband, "We did it! I didn't die, and I did something I never imagined I would ever do. Jon, could it be that God is calling us to something new?"

It should not have surprised me that this experience happened when I was pregnant with my third child. We named him David after Jon's Uncle David. David Isaiah is my prophet and king. When Jon and I found out we were having a third child, we prayerfully considered a number of names, but David kept coming back to us. We wanted this child to be full of life, to love to laugh, and to understand that our God is a God of at least seventeen chances. We wanted our son to understand that God isn't through with us when we walk away or even run but that God patiently waits for us to grow into fully human versions of ourselves. Ironic, isn't it, that my seventeenth chance would come when I was birthing new-life possibilities for my family—when I was giving birth to David. When I take a thirty-thousand-foot view of my life, I think, *God, you've taken my mess and turned it into a beautiful miracle.*

When we give fierce room enough to quiet down fear, we open our lives up to new dreams and possibilities. I couldn't see my future possibilities from my fear-soaked rut. Fierce fueled in my heart and mind images of new, wild dreams for our future. It's kind of like Mario Brothers 3. One of the interesting features of this Nintendo video game, popular in the 1990s, was that you could not see the path ahead of you. Each time you completed a level in the game, the dark screen would reveal the next right move you needed to make. I am sure some tech-savvy teenagers were able to hack their way around this feature, but for game commoners like myself, I had to move level by level, always getting just enough light to make my next right move. That's how I feel life is like when it comes to discovering our meaning and purpose. We don't get the whole path. We are not given the entire road map of our future. We are given choices and opportunities, and lots of them. It's not one and done. Even if we really want to complete the game, it's not about winning; it's about the growth we experience at every level.

There is room in our lives for error, and there is room in our lives for no. Sometimes it is okay to say no, even out of fear. But no does not mean never. It does not mean that full-life opportunities will never come again; it just means that there is some fierce to be developed in the face of fear. I wish someone would have told my twenty-some-year-old self, "It's okay to not always get life right. You will have another opportunity!" Sometimes so-called faith-filled people act as if we don't have time, as though time is a resource we can't afford to lose. When taken to the extreme, we live in a frantic panic, acting as if our timely decisions are mission-critical for the world's well-being. But this chronic hustle is just another form of control, and I am not in control. You are not in control. Faith-filled people have a lot of time. So what would it look like for you and me to develop fierce in the face of fear and suffering? That's the work, that's the job, to discover, uncover a power and presence that God freely pours over us. We have the work of developing fierce over time, over a lifetime, in fact.

Mary had many opportunities to develop her own form of fierce when she asked her son to perform a miracle at a wedding in Cana. The bride's family was facing social disaster, and in order to save the day and their reputation, Jesus turned the water into wine. He didn't want to, he said he wasn't ready, but Mary insisted, and Jesus did what his mama asked.

But what about the times when she asked for him and he said, "Who is my mother?" And certainly her fierce wavered when she was looking up at her son hanging on the cross. But God had made Mary a promise, not a guarantee. This purpose, this calling for Mary, wasn't easy. Everything she ever feared about this holy son of hers came true. His presence, his power, his way of turning the world inside out and upside down got him crucified. This was not what Mary had signed up for, and yet it was everything the messenger had promised. Standing at the foot of the cross, watching her son die a terrible death, was more fear and grief than any one mother should have to carry. But then, in what seemed like a final act of care and compassion, Jesus saw his mother, saw her fear and her pain, and made a way for her future. "When Jesus saw his mother there, and the disciple whom he loved standing nearby, he said to her, 'Woman, here is your son,' and to the disciple, 'Here is your mother.' From that time on, this disciple took her into his home" (John 19:26-27).

I would be pretending if I said I am no longer afraid. Fear has always been something that I face nearly every day of my life. But I once had someone advise me about the place of fear in deciding about my purpose and call: "Think about your choices. Which choice scares you the most? You know the one. If you say yes to that choice, you think, *There's no way this will work. I can't do it. It's beyond my skills and gifts.* Well that's what purpose feels like. It's terrifying, it's beyond your capacity. It's beyond you! That's the kind of decision you need to say yes to—that's a God opportunity."

When I think about a challenging opportunity that I am facing, and the thought makes me want to puke, that's probably a God opportunity. But if I am pondering an opportunity with the thought, *I could do that with my eyes closed,* I'd better reexamine whether that is the right yes for me. I wish fierce and fear could coexist with harmony in my head, but they don't. Oh, don't misunderstand what I am saying—they are both present in my mind. But they don't leave room for each other. Either I will be led by fear or led by fierce. They don't make great dancing partners. But don't worry, we all have time to choose fierce.

So What?

When thinking about the story of your life, what were your defining moments? Were they during a "sanitized" time in your life, or did they happen smack-dab in the middle of a mess?

Do you believe your life purpose includes all of you? You are a fully embodied person. What fears do you need to overcome?

Do you have fear-soaked ruts in your head that shape your daily decisions? How can you make room for fierce and put fear in its proper place?

What real-life decisions are in front of you? What's your reaction to the yes? To the no? Is this a God opportunity?

~ 7 ~

FACING THE PHARAOH

*Moses answered, "What if they do not believe me or listen
to me and say, 'The Lord did not appear to you?'" Then
the Lord said to him, "What is that in your hand?"*

Exodus 4:1-2

Moses seemed to have a pretty good gig. This Hebrew-slave-turned-Egyptian-prince enjoyed all the wealth of Egypt with a continued connection with his family roots. Moses navigated both worlds well, until one day he saw the cruelty of the Egyptian taskmasters unleashed on a fellow Hebrew, and he snapped. Moses murdered the Egyptian and ran into the wilderness to evade punishment.

Although I can draw all kinds of conclusions about why Moses ran, the most compelling reason is fear. Moses was afraid for his life. "When Pharaoh heard of this, he tried to kill Moses, but Moses fled from Pharaoh and went to live in Midian, where he sat down by a well" (Exodus 2:15). Moses could no longer deny the identity of his past, and he seemed powerless to create a healthy future within the boundaries of Egypt. Wandering in the wilderness, Moses stumbled upon the sheep of the priest of Midian. Moses's kindness and charisma won the heart of his future father-in-law, Jethro, securing his employment, a wife, and a place at the family table. For a while, Moses was able to evade the demons of his past and create a peaceful future among the sheep and shepherds.

> Just because you experience moments of courage in the face of injustice does not mean that you are ready to overturn the entire Egyptian world order.

I sometimes wonder if Moses ever missed his past. Of course, there were the riches of Egypt, the education, the influence. But there were also the relationships with the people he loved. His adoptive mother was a princess in Egypt. What about her grief? She probably grieved not only because her son had run away from the wrath of her father the Pharaoh but also because she couldn't ignore her son's deep identity as a Hebrew. Moses didn't just murder an Egyptian; it seemed that Moses had chosen sides. He had reclaimed his identity as one of his people—the people of God.

Normally I wouldn't use a murder to illustrate a positive turning point in someone's life. But Moses's violence against the Egyptian led to justice for God's people. Moses fought for God's people and not his own personal happiness. For the first time in his life, Moses's purpose was bigger than himself. His mission was beyond Moses! Maybe, just maybe, Moses wasn't running from the fear of death but rather from his life's mission. The death of the Egyptian signaled to God's people, to Pharaoh, and to Moses himself that he was willing to fight back. This person of influence was willing to fight for the justice of those who were being oppressed.

Moses became a threat to the Egyptian lifestyle, to the social order, and to Pharaoh's Egypt. Pharaoh's Egypt and order were maintained with a particular social and religious worldview. The people on top of the social ladder maintained all the power, and those on the bottom were used, abused, and oppressed. Beyond rule-breaking, Moses topped the social order, and that warranted Moses's death. Moses was called to boldly fight for God's people, to turn Pharaoh's Egypt upside down and inside out!

Those who find fierce do not maintain the status quo, ignore social injustice, or ignore opportunities to overturn the powers that insist on maintaining a world order that keeps entire groups oppressed. But just because you experience moments of courage in the face of injustice does not mean that you are ready to overturn the entire Egyptian world order. Particularly not when you believe your entire life, identity, and livelihood were created by the system.

We are constantly conditioned not to rock the boat, to create harmony in the workplace, and to make sure that those in power maintain their power. We are conditioned to be anything but fierce. Not much has changed about the human condition from the time of Moses's and Pharaoh's Egypt: power, greed, and our tendency to use people and systems to get what we want and what we think we need still dominate the political landscape. Although one wouldn't characterize all of United States politics to be like Pharaoh's Egypt, it's not difficult to draw parallels. We order our lives around the social myth that Pharaoh and his cronies somehow deserve to be at the top of the social ladder, and that wealth and success warrant a social status that the rest of us just don't deserve. We maintain the social status quo because if we do not, it would point out the major flaws in this line of thinking.

Our social theology maintains that those who are on top deserve to be on top, and those who are on the bottom earned their spot on the bottom. It's a social caste system, and the lie of our U.S. experience is that anyone in the U.S. can break these barriers and rise to another level on the social ladder. We love a great underdog story, and that's the fierce that our culture is selling. But Moses's breed of fierce isn't an underdog story. Sure, he was born a slave and became an Egyptian prince, but what led Moses to his purpose was not a climb to the top but rather a social death-bomb to the bottom. Moses sided with the oppressed and the very people God was already siding with. Fierce led Moses to realize that his life's purpose was bigger than himself.

> I am called to face the Pharaoh, not to tend the sheep. I may be filled with excuses, but I cannot allow those excuses to keep me and the people around me from stepping into God's promised future.

But Moses was afraid. Afraid of his future, afraid of facing his past, and afraid to do something beyond the limitations of his personal life experiences. It's in that state of fear that Moses found himself face to face with the God of the universe. Moses was minding his own business, tending his father-in-law's sheep, when he noticed something peculiar on the side of a mountain: a bush on fire that wasn't being burned up. His curiosity led Moses to the place where he would encounter God.

When the Lord *saw that he had gone over to look,*
God called to him from within the bush, "Moses! Moses!"
And Moses said, "Here I am." "Do not come any closer,"
God said. "Take off your sandals, for the place where
you are standing is holy ground." Then he said, "I am
the God of your father, the God of Abraham, the God of
Isaac and the God of Jacob." At this, Moses hid his face,
because he was afraid to look at God.

Exodus 3:4-6

Tradition in the Old Testament stated that if a person looked at God, he or she would die. But Moses did not die; instead, Moses was anointed leader and deliverer of God's people. How did Moses respond to this cosmic assignment? Fear. Moses was afraid and responded to God with a line of thoughtful excuses: "I am not good enough," "I don't have all the answers," "People will not believe me," "I can't speak," and "I am not qualified" (Exodus 3:11, 3:13, 4:1, 4:10, 4:13).

Most of us human types can find our own excuses in this list. On the surface, they may seem like a humble response to such a monumental task, but look at Moses's résumé. There was a reason Moses was plucked from the river and placed into the arms of an Egyptian princess. Moses had an Egyptian education. His resourcefulness led him to survive the wilderness. His charisma and compassion gave him an in with his father-in-law. And he quickly and easily stepped right into leading the family sheepherding business. Moses was no slouch in the wilderness.

God had prepared Moses for leadership, but Moses didn't want to face the pain and difficulty that this level of leadership warranted. Moses wanted the comfort of the field over the conflict with Pharaoh. How many times in our lives do we believe that

God is calling us to more? God is asking us to defy Pharaoh's Egypt, to rock the boat, to make people uncomfortable; but, in reply, we give God a handful of excuses. "God, I couldn't. I am not qualified! No one would take me seriously! I don't even know those people, God! How could you ever use me for something that big? Let me stay right where I am. I know these sheep; these sheep know me. This is a pretty good gig, God. I am good right where I am. Thanks, God, but no thanks!"

Fearful Excuses

I side with Moses. It's easy on this side of the story to think that Moses was being some kind of spiritual whiner. *I mean, come on, Moses. God has never visited me through the supernatural flames of a bush that didn't burn up.* But as I read through Moses's story, I realize that being chosen comes with a price. Moses was called to sacrifice his quiet life in the mountains among the sheep to shepherd millions of former slaves into a land that God had promised them. Getting the people out of Egypt would be the easy part; getting Egypt out of the people would be much harder. If Moses knew the challenges he faced, no wonder he was full of excuses. I know that I am.

When face to face with people challenges, I want to run. When life gets hard and leadership decisions become challenging, I find myself wanting to run to what I know rather than facing God's preferred future unafraid. Like Moses, I want to stay with the sheep. Okay, I am not a shepherd, but every time I feel like the mission is beyond me, I tend to start daydreaming about our family farm. I grew up on a farm in the hills of Hocking County. It's a beautiful place to live, where the pace is more relaxed and the atmosphere heavenly. When the fireflies come out at night and spread themselves throughout the fields, the sight nearly takes your breath away. I want to live that simple life. Farming is not a bad gig, but I find myself romanticizing the past. The farm is beautiful, the life comfortable, and the task straightforward—or at least it is in my mind!

But let's be honest: it's been nearly twenty years since I lived on the farm. Today, I would make a terrible farmer! But I daydream about the farm because I want to escape the present. *I can't do this, God! I am only a farmer at heart. I am not smart enough, experienced enough, male enough, driven enough, old enough, you-name-your-excuse enough to do this! This is beyond my pay grade! Besides the family farm is safe and is something I know!* Those daydreams last for a moment and then I snap back into reality. *Rachel, really? You are going to plant a garden? You can't even keep your houseplants alive! You want to go back and haul manure and bale hay? Sure, Rachel, so why, when you have to pack water from the house to the barn in winter, do you realize, "Nope, I am not meant to be a farmer"?*

In that moment, I realize I can't go back. I am called to face the Pharaoh, not to tend the sheep. I may be filled with excuses, but I cannot allow those excuses to keep me and the people around me from stepping into God's promised future. I've got to let the fear and excuses go! And although I can fiercely face nearly every excuse that crops up in my mind, there's one excuse that keeps me from leading fierce: "But, God, what if people don't like me?"

I Love Being Loved

Moses wrestled with this one. He had no idea how he was going to get God's people to like him, let alone follow him out of Egypt and into the Promised Land. I get it, Moses, I love to be loved. It's the shadow side of having an achiever's strength, coupled with a healthy dose of competition. But fierce doesn't allow for love in all situations. Oh, don't get me wrong, God loves me. But when I have to face the fact that another human being might not like me, let alone love me or even want to be on my team, it's not just hurtful; that kind of rejection can be devastating.

Fierce doesn't allow for mediocre excuses like, "Well if I say that, they might get upset. What if what I say hurts that person's feelings?" Or the worst, "What if so-and-so doesn't like me?" I like to compete, but sometimes folks misunderstand my desire for competition with a cutthroat drive to win. I don't like to win when I am the only person left standing. Life is a team sport for me.

I thrive in hard-charging, high-expectation, lay-your-sword-on-the-table environments; but when others don't want to win, when they don't want to compete, I don't want them on my team. That means having really hard conversations. When I have to have a hard conversation with a staff person, family member, or friend, I've got to work myself into it. It's not difficult when people are eager to be coached, but when someone thinks that they are thriving and they are not, or when someone's self-awareness is limited, it's an extremely painful process for me. Why? Because most likely it will cost me. I will lose my status as the one who is loved.

Can I be tough in the moment? You bet I can! But what happens when you are in a deep relationship with a person, and you realize you've got to say some stuff that's going to make that person upset? Do you ignore it and pretend it's going to go away? Do you run from the hard conversation? Do you bury it until you can't bury it any longer? Do you leave the organization that you love, or do you put on your big boy pants, march right in, and speak the truth in love? In his letter to the Ephesians, Paul said,

> *Then we will no longer be infants, tossed back and forth by the waves, and blown here and there by every wind of teaching and by the cunning and craftiness of people in their deceitful scheming. Instead, speaking the truth in love, we will grow to become in every respect the mature body of him who is the head, that is, Christ. From him the whole body, joined and held together by every supporting ligament, grows and builds itself up in love, as each part does its work.*
>
> *Ephesians 4:14-16*

In other words, grow up! Hard conversations are a vital part of what it means to lead out of our fierce. I hope if you have any dreams of leading the human race into our future, you grab onto the courage to speak the truth in love.

Tough Love

Speaking truth in love is not easy. I remember the first hard conversation I had to have with a staff person. Walking into my office, I was poised on the outside—professional and ready with my bulleted list of growing edges. But on the inside, I wanted to run, puke, and scream, "I don't want to do this!" I could feel the tension rising in my neck. Speaking truth with love is the only way to rightly understand yourself in healthy relationships with others. But lovingly speaking truth is not a skill that most humans learn in their families of origin and certainly not through routine paths of education. No, our formation into adulthood is about conforming, keeping our noses clean, sitting in our seats, and being obedient to what all those in authority are telling us. It's propping up Pharaoh's Egypt. Folks on top of the system are there for a reason, and you and I are called to stay in our lane! But all that conformity fails to engage us in regular healthy conflict. Conflict helps us all understand, embrace, and employ our differences for a common, unifying mission. It's not about letting folks do what they want. Speaking the truth in love allows people to grow into our God destiny.

So I walk into the room sick with worry, my stomach in knots, determined to get in and out as quickly as possible. There is no way that I am ripping off the professional bandage slowly. My first victim didn't even see it coming. I am sure I could have done a better job of giving critical feedback along the way, but no, I preferred to stuff it all until I dropped the hammer and said, "You are no longer a fit for this team." Courageous? No, waiting to speak truth is not a courageous, helpful, or even healthy form of management. I watched as the person's face changed from that all-too-familiar smile to surprise and then disbelief. They didn't say it, but I could hear, "But, Rachel, I thought we were friends!" The conversation ended and we all walked out of the meeting with a grab bag of hurt feelings.

It was in this moment that I wanted to walk out of the meeting and not come back. I hadn't signed up for this. No one had told me that hard, painful conversations were in the job contract.

As a child, I'd had these visions of life being a series of summer camp experiences. Oh yeah, there would be conflict—so-and-so liking so-and-so's girl—but by the end of the day we'd all be singing "Kumbaya" around the campfire. *News flash, Rachel. Not every episode of your life story ends in forty-two minutes with the conflict thoroughly resolved.*

Conflict is good, healthy, natural. Human beings were designed to grow and not to stay the same. Certainly, I see the physical growth in my own children. But growth is not merely physical. There is an entire gift of growing relationally, emotionally, and spiritually that I realize I've barely tapped into because I, like Moses, lead with excuses. "But, God, what if that person was deeply hurt by what I said and blames me for that hurt?" On the surface, it may seem admirable to want to be kind to people, but when those relationships become a stumbling block to your future health or the future health of your organization, it's time to wake up, look in the mirror, and say, "Rachel, you can't always be loved!" Besides, God's preferred picture and mission for the world aren't all about you.

It's Personal

Maybe you learned this lesson in fierce way before I learned it. Too often I took every criticism, email, and comment personally. I've got an incredible memory, which is great for memorizing presentations, but not when you have a systematic file of every terrible thing another human did or said to you. How do you handle the threats to your identity, your purpose, and leadership? Sometimes you need perspective from someone who is a little wiser, a little more seasoned, and a whole lot more popular than you.

My epiphany about my tendency to want people to love me came from a preacher—I know, crazy, right? Bishop T. D. Jakes preached a sermon called "Combustible Passion," at the 2010

Leadership Summit. Right there, the man saved my career and my calling. He asked the question, "How do we help people operate out of their passion?" He reminded us that people don't come to the church to follow us but to follow Jesus. "People come to follow Jesus, and they are stuck with you!"[1]

We create this strange spiritual codependence with our people. We want people to like us, and many of us want people to love us! Just look at how often you check your social media posts to see if anyone has liked, loved, or commented on them. Yeah, we are obsessed. Bishop Jakes talked about our tendency as human beings to think that people need to be our confidants "for us!" We expect everyone in our organization to have passion for us. This is a really human response, but Bishop Jakes opened my mind to a wider organization principle: "Most people in your organization are constituents. Constituents are not for you; they are people who are for what you are for." These are the folks who are part of the mission because they are passionate about the mission—not passionate about you. That leadership principle alone saved my life, but what he described next would give me the tools that I needed to discover my fierce in every aspect of my purpose and to rightly align my professional relationships.

Bishop Jakes went on to say, "People who are for you are confidants. And you will be lucky to have a handful of confidants in your lifetime." The truth was, in that moment of my life, I expected *everybody* to be for me: for me as a leader, as a pastor, and as the person who would bring personal transformation to their lives. Of course, nearly every person in my church was supposed to be for me.

But Bishop Jakes reminded me that every time someone left the church or the ministry I was a part of, I took it personally.

I felt as though that person or group of people had left *me*. They hadn't! They were never for me in the first place! They were for what I was for. This was the real game-changer for me: people are not and were not created to be for me. Life is not some kind of massive popularity contest. No matter the number of likes on Facebook, number of Instagram followers, or popularity of my tweets, people are meant to have a common cause—not a common confidant. My purpose is so much bigger than myself!

In that moment, I realized I had misinterpreted the world around me. The role I played in my organization was not to get people to be for me, to love me, to affirm me as a leader, but to inspire people to be for what I was for. It might sound simple, but suddenly I had a whole new perspective on those conversations and comments that I had taken so personally. People are supposed to be for what I am for—that knowledge, that nugget of organizational truth, set me up to find my fierce in a way I had never found fierce before! For the first time, I was free to lead without carrying around the baggage of beloved popularity. I didn't have to be loved.

Fierce Tested

Developing fierce leadership does not happen with one courageous epiphany or decision. We come face to face with many opportunities that test and challenge the fierce within. Growing into fierce is a process just like earning trust.

In one organization that I was part of for a while, I thought I was doing a decent job of earning trust, doing everything I thought I needed to: having the hard conversations, calling people out who needed to be, and following up when things didn't end well. What I was really doing was acting out of fierce.

Our organization was in a season of transition, and it seemed urgent that I solidify my colleagues' trust in my leadership. A meeting with my supervisor and nearly all of my direct reports was deemed the quickest way to achieve this. During the meeting, each of my reports would be given the opportunity to provide feedback about my leadership. The meeting wasn't formal or scheduled, however, and as a result, wasn't the healthiest of experiences. This was a gripe session. Our organization was prime for conflict and professional tipping points, and I just happened to take the brunt of one of those moments.

The meeting was an hour and a half of all that I was doing to fail these leaders, the organization, and the future momentum of the movement. It's not every day that you experience professional crucifixion. I listened, talked when I believed it necessary, and after a while, realized that this would be a personal turning point for me within the organization. Finally, the meeting was over, and I left the room confused, deflated, in tears, and full of pain. I hadn't recognized their dissatisfaction with me. Something would have to change. There was a real-life decision in front of me: run from the unhealthiness of this moment or fiercely lead my way out of it.

In that moment, I wanted to run. The pain seemed too real, the damage too deep in order to maintain any composure of professional leadership. But I also knew that I had changed. No longer was I obsessed with being loved. I knew I had to filter through the comments and not respond out of emotion but rather out of principle. The experience tested my fierce: would I run back to a world where I could be loved or would I lead my way out of this organizational mess? In this moment, which I call my leadership 360, I chose to lead.

Leading began with giving myself space to think and to plan. I knew I was in a position to react out of sheer emotion. I love emotion, but I do not want to be controlled by my emotions. I want to respond out of fierce identity rather than reactive emotion. So I went home and gave myself the evening to feel sorry for myself, to grieve my own personal blind spots, to mourn the loss of relationship, and also to say right out loud, "That sucked!" Then I remembered that God doesn't promise that my life will be easy or my purpose smooth-sailing. So, the very next day, I decided I needed help. I needed perspective. I needed Tim.

Everybody Needs a Tim

Tim Schoonover has been one of the few confidants I have had. Tim is genuinely for me. Professionally, I knew that Tim could give me perspective on what I had experienced.

Tim serves as the owner and CEO of Promark, an outplacement company that specializes in leadership transitions and career coaching. He also happens to be clergy in the United Methodist Church. With words of professional and spiritual wisdom, he could move my gaze beyond the weeds of hurt onto possibilities for the future.

"Rachel, I am sorry," he said. "I don't want you to have these painful experiences. And you have every reason to leave this organization, but don't just run from something. Make sure you have something to run to before you leave." In that moment, I knew Tim was right. I had every reason to leave, but also every reason to stay.

"If I stay, Tim, what on earth am I going to do to regain the trust of the people around me?" I demanded.

"I'm glad you asked." Tim said.

My blinders were off and I was going to have to do the hard work of leading the way out of a leadership deficit. It would take work, but it was work I was willing to do. Tim and I spent the afternoon dreaming up a leadership strategy, which would start with my affirming what I had heard in the meeting: those growing edges to my leadership that people had voiced out loud. But our strategy would also give me the opportunity to name what I believed to be unhealthy organizational practices. I committed myself to more effective communication, further accessibility, and frank discussion. I let my team know I wasn't going anywhere, but that I would lead out of the mess that I found myself in.

Too often I have believed the lie that leaders are born with every leadership principle they need in their heads and hearts. I do believe that some folks have natural giftings that make them better suited for leadership, but I also believe that fierce leadership is developed over time. It is experience that shapes and defines your leadership. Just as it is experience that shapes and defines your fierce.

What Happens When You Stay

When face to face with God, Moses had a courageous decision to make. But this would be only the first in a series of courageous decisions he would have to make. Years later, when the mission changed from delivering the people out of Egypt to preparing them for the Promised Land, on more than one occasion, Moses reminded God that he "hadn't signed up for this!" Daily frustrations mounted for Moses, until Moses questioned God's purpose for his life and the lives of God's people.

And Moses said to the Lord, "Why are you treating me, your servant, so harshly? Have mercy on me! What did I do to deserve the burden of all these people? Did I give birth to them? Did I bring them into the world? Why did you tell me to carry them in my arms like a mother carries a nursing baby? How can I carry them to the land you swore to give their ancestors? Where am I supposed to get meat for all these people? They keep whining to me, saying, 'Give us meat to eat!' I can't carry all these people by myself! The load is far too heavy! If this is how you intend to treat me, just go ahead and kill me. Do me a favor and spare me this misery!"

Numbers 11:11-15 NLT

And as if Moses wasn't already under enough pressure, most of the time, the people grumbled against Moses and his leadership. This should be no surprise. People will say some terrible things about you, especially if you are leading fiercely. I'll never forget a letter that I received several years ago, just after I had left a position. Someone had anonymously handwritten a note. On the note, they taped two pennies and wrote, "My two cents." In the letter, they described what a terrible leader I had been. Although I don't remember all the details, I do remember the line where the person called me the "spawn of Satan." That is a pretty bold description of a pastor.

A word of advice about offering critical feedback: sign the note with your real name, or better yet, have the conversation face to face. In a culture where people are encouraged to cower behind the keyboard, there is something fierce about talking with another face to face. We owe one another the honor and respect of sharing our concerns and frustrations in a manner that brings dignity. We are not called to demonize; we are called to speak the truth in love—and that is a lot easier when you are face to face with the person.

Now in a former life, I would have taken this note personally, but I was finally at a place where I could put that into the mental category it needed to go into: unhealthy grief. Perhaps that person was disappointed with my leaving, perhaps they took my leaving as an opportunity to give me a piece of their mind, or perhaps I just happened to be the perfect scapegoat for their years of disappointment in pastoral leadership. Whatever the case, I put those two pennies in the offering plate and threw away the letter.

Most of the time, notes like these aren't about me. Instead, they reflect the very real pain of the person writing them. Likewise, the people's grumbling wasn't about Moses.

Moses had been the one called to lead God's people out of slavery and into the Promised Land, but the mission had never been about Moses, and it certainly wasn't about Moses's popularity. God gave Moses the assignment because God wanted to deliver God's people—period! Fierce means developing people who are for what you are for, even if that means they are not necessarily for you.

When You Are in the Hot Seat

Since I seem to learn everything the hard way, I began my professional career bristling at every piece of professional criticism I received. I am an achiever who is always working toward high marks, but when I miss the mark, I can quickly fall into a professional panic. I have had to learn over the years to work toward receiving criticism with an open hand.

Why an open hand? If I am open-handed, then it is impossible for me to be immediately defensive. When my hands are open, the posture alone helps remind me to open my ears, eyes, mind, and heart to what the other person is saying. But the open hand is not just a posture of receiving; it's also a posture of letting go. An open hand allows me to evaluate the criticism I'm receiving and to determine if it is helpful and constructive. If it is not, then the open hand allows me to let it go. Constructive feedback is vital to growing our fierce. Don't be afraid of it, don't ignore it, but don't hold onto it either. The open hand helps us to receive what needs to be received, to let go of what needs to be let go, and to proactively move into God's preferred future for our lives.

As I have worked my way through my professional fears, excuses, and frustrations, it has not all been smooth, and I certainly didn't make all the right professional moves. But over the years, like Moses, I have grown and realized that my professional purpose and calling is way beyond me. Our journey to fierce not only affects our lives but has long-lasting effects on the lives of others. Our purpose is bigger than ourselves!

Since the Israelites aren't the only people to whom God promised a future, you and I also get to be a part of fiercely leading the folks in our circle of influence into their promised futures. But we must remember that Moses's journey into fierce leadership came with a price. He had to be willing to let go of his comfortable shepherding lifestyle and lead God's people into the Promised Land.

I don't know what Moses's God is asking you to face, but I know this: fierce leadership comes with a price. What are you going to give up in order to step into the future that God is calling you to lead? Do not be led by your fears or excuses. There is an entire world of people waiting for you to let go of your excuses and to step into fierce.

So What?

Think back over your personal and professional career. What are your "go to" excuses when you are confronted with your own weakness or failure?

Have you ever had to have hard conversations with people? When have you failed to tell someone the truth about a situation?

Have people ever had to have hard conversations with you? How did you respond? When have you taken criticism personally? Can you reimagine a path for receiving that constructive feedback?

Can you name the people in your life who are for you? Do you have a Tim?

What is happening in your organization? Do you need to redefine your leadership? What would it take to lead your way out of a leadership deficit?

Make a plan to fiercely grow your leadership!

8

SOMETIMES SILENT

*Now a man of the tribe of Levi married a Levite woman,
and she became pregnant and gave birth to a son. When
she saw that he was a fine child, she hid him for three
months.*

Exodus 2:1-2

It's a family affair—hiding Moses, that is, and remaining silent so that this special baby boy could stay alive. I've given birth and raised four children through the infant stage, and when I think of the challenges that Moses's mother and father must have faced to keep their precious child alive, it nearly takes my breath away. Each cry, every whimper, moment by moment wondering if the family would be exposed. Keeping children alive in those early stages is a grab bag of fears; I can't imagine adding strict silence in the face of genocide to the mix.

Silent—that's what the child needed to be in order to keep the family alive. But aren't hiding and silence threats to the family's future health? Could silence eradicate the intimacy and vulnerability that's necessary for a family to be, well, a family? How many future family conversations (or counseling sessions) would be necessary to work through the kind of trauma that such silence created? Certainly, I can understand these are extreme circumstances—the threat of death, the desire for life. Could it be that this kind of silence is a unique opportunity for fierce? The hiding and silence weren't so much tools employed to keep family pain buried but rather survival tactics to maintain life—a special young life.

My Uncle Mick and I were the best of friends. Although he was much older than I was, he was as youthful as they come. Oh, and funny! It seemed everywhere my uncle went, crowds gathered around him to listen to his stories. He could tell a good story, with loads of dramatic, nearly theatrical, flare, making seemingly insignificant details come to life as he built the story up to the punchline. Then, at just the right time, he would throw his head back and laugh, his joy too contagious not to prompt others to join in.

My uncle was the kind of uncle every kid wanted: kind, fun, and generous. He was impossible not to love. My affinity for my uncle came because he treated me specially. We were both middle children, and, to him, that meant we were "the best-looking, smartest, and most misunderstood." My uncle got me, he loved me, and I cherished every moment I spent with him. Besides, he was my favorite! Very few people in this world fell into that category. I know we aren't supposed to have favorites, but I did. First my Grandma Ruby and then, after her death, my Uncle Mick.

During college summers, we worked together, and sometimes I spent the night at his house so I didn't have to drive back to my house before work the next day. We even socialized together, whether traveling to flea markets—Mick had a ravenous appetite for "old things"—or attending dinner parties where we would have fancy drinks and eat his favorite

French onion soup. I can still see his smile as he delighted over the melted cheese that crusted around the bowl! Mick was my friend, my confidant, my person. And in a real way, I was kind of his. I mean, I was just a kid, barely having graduated high school. I certainly couldn't understand the complexities of his adult life. But I am sure there was something refreshing about my unconditional love for my uncle.

Mick knew who I was—it was clear even then that I followed Jesus and wanted to live my life for and in vocation with the movement of God. He also knew that I grew up in a home that, by most standards, would be considered conservative, spiritually and politically. But he also knew that I loved him no matter what. I did love my uncle no matter what. My love for him wasn't based on his church attendance or even the life that he chose to live. I just knew my uncle was "good people" and the kind of "good people" I wanted to spend my free time with. But, oh, dear reader, there is a bit of family history that you might need to know for all of this story to be clear.

I think I was eleven years old, sitting at the kitchen table with my older brother, Jason. My mom had asked us to sit down because she wanted to tell us something very important. She was nervous, pacing the floor. Words struggled to topple over her lips. "I really don't know how to say this to you," Mom stammered. We rolled our eyes.

"What, Mom? Just say it."

"Well, your Uncle Mick is, is, is . . . he's gay," she said, as if dropping the most salacious news a parent could ever drop on two kids.

"Yeah, Mom, we know," my brother said.

"Isn't it obvious?" I said, my remarks dripped with confidence and sarcasm.

I am not sure we really knew. We just knew our uncle was different. He was animated, he loved to decorate, and he had a lot of guy friends who frequently hung around. In our young, maybe even sheltered, minds, he fit some of our homosexual stereotypes. I couldn't tell if my mom was relieved or horrified.

"You knew?" she questioned. "How did you know?"

Next came a torrent of questions and what I considered a paranoid misunderstanding about homosexuality.

"Have you seen things?" she asked. "Has your uncle ever done anything weird in front of you?"

"Really, Mom!" we protested. But she was my mom and, in her mind, she wanted to protect us. We spent so much time with my uncle. He loved each one of us—my brother, sister, and me—as though we were his own. It was clear that she didn't approve of his "lifestyle," but to her and my father's credit, that didn't keep them from loving Mick either. Although they may have openly hoped for a different life for Mick, it was never meant to be. And who could blame them? We lived in a small town, with a limited perspective on this kind of thing. At the time, most gay people living near us were not open about their sexuality; to be so, in the words of my uncle, "would get your ass kicked." I grew up with the knowledge that my uncle was gay but did not witness a lot of evidence that he was open about it.

So when we became besties, I realized that my uncle had "come out of the closet," but only to those he deemed safe enough to know the real Mick. It was fascinating to watch my uncle navigate the world. He wasn't a man's man, but he wouldn't shy away from making comments about a woman's physique or even telling jokes that would lead one to believe that his heterosexual tendencies were in full swing. Humor was how my uncle thrived and survived his life. His stories saved him. He was hiding, right out in the open, but hiding to stay alive or at least not to experience total social death.

When, in the summer of 2000, my uncle asked me to go on vacation with him, I said yes! We traveled to Lake Erie for a weekend of camping, and it was there that I encountered some of my uncle's friends. We took a boat ride with two couples, all of them men, and some who fit nicely into the definition of what I thought it meant to be gay. But then there was another guy—let's call him Pat. Pat and his partner, Ron, had been together for nearly thirty years. And Pat looked more like a friendly grandpa than someone who was gay: his ball cap, blue jeans, and warm demeanor all seemed really, really "normal." *How is this guy gay?* I wondered.

On that day, I received an education about the kind of generalized stereotypes that I like to paint people with; I get that I had a limited worldview, but I kind of liked "knowing things," took pride in knowing things, and thought I had navigated the wider world of knowing things pretty well. Nope! My uncle opened my eyes to a picture of his world that I had never seen, and it kind of wrecked me. Perhaps it was because I'd had strong convictions about sex and sexuality that were more traditional by nature, but it may also have been because I had discovered there was a world of people who existed far beyond my worldview. When I stepped off the boat, I felt dizzy, and it was from more than the rum and coke. I knew relationships changed perspective, but this—this shook me and helped me realize that judgment is still judgment in whatever well-meaning package it comes in.

But my experience with Pat wouldn't be the only thing that week that would challenge my worldview.

The Secret

The week ended, and soon we were on our way back home when my uncle asked me a question. "Can you keep a secret?"

"A secret?" I laughed. I figured Mick was going to tell me some juicy piece of gossip or even about someone that he secretly or not-so-secretly had a crush on.

"No, really, can you keep a secret?" he said.

"Yeah, sure."

"Your Grandma Ruby was the keeper of my secret. She made sure that I would be okay. She knew what I needed her to do if I got sick or if something happened. So, now that she has died, Rachel, I am asking you to now keep the secret."

What he said made me feel like a cross between the priest in the midst of hearing a confession and an FBI agent handling his "case." But if Mick trusted his mom, my grandma, with the secret, I knew it was serious. Mick knew that I loved her, maybe even idolized her, and that I would be eager to keep the tradition of holding *this* secret.

The silence didn't feel like a burden but rather a calling, a purpose. Like Miriam, Moses's sister, standing on the edge of the Nile river, I was protecting the special one.

"Well, if you put it that way, absolutely! I would be honored to keep your secret," I said.

Then, with something that can only be described as a grieving confidence, Mick said, "I am HIV-positive." Those words hung in the air like a thick fog. I felt their weight.

They were like a sucker punch to the gut. I don't know what I was expecting my uncle to say, but that wasn't it. He went on for what seemed to be hours, talking about how he'd known he was different as a kid.

"I was never really attracted to women," he said. "I tried to be like the other boys, but I wasn't." The runt of his family, Mick was small, something like thirty-two pounds when he started school in the first grade. Kids made fun of him, so he knew the pain of teasing, but he also knew the pain of being different—very different.

"I wanted God to take this away from me," he said. "I would pray and pray and pray. I even tried to commit suicide a few times, but it just didn't work." Mick had once had a relationship with a man that he'd hoped would last a lifetime, and when it didn't, he landed in the arms of someone who didn't tell him until it was too late that he was HIV positive.

I have to be honest: when he told me that last bit, I was angry, and my uncle could tell it.

"Rachel, it was the late eighties," he explained. "People didn't know they were positive, and many were too scared to tell anyone. It's not worth getting mad about." It seemed a little strange to me that Mick could have this level of compassion and grace. Clearly there were demons that he had already worked through.

"It's why I take so many pills," he said. "So far, so good. Many of the people I knew who got it when I did are already dead, so I feel pretty lucky." *Lucky?* I thought.

"Rachel, here's what you really need to know. If I get sick, if I go to the hospital, I will call you, and you will be able to talk to the doctors on my behalf. I need someone to know the truth. Someone to advocate for me," Mick said.

That I could do! I could hold my uncle's secret in my heart, in my head, and in my hands. I could and would be his advocate. I would help him hide and remain silent so that he could stay alive. That's what I wanted for my uncle—life!

> Christians are water people. Water tells our story. I can imagine my uncle waiting for the waters of baptism to trickle over his head, with the words of God's story spoken over his life.

All things considered, I would have much rather Mick been honest and open, and let everyone know the pain and fear he carried. But, as he explained, at least in that moment, "that just wasn't possible." So, I became the secret-bearer, his partner in hiding and silence. My family, his family, did not know. I didn't want to treat him differently, and I didn't want my family to treat him differently.

Family secrets are interesting, aren't they? Most of the time they carry with them pain and half-truths. The same was true for this one. But not in the same way as some family secrets. Even if I avoided talking with my family about Mick's secret, I wouldn't avoid talking to Mick. I wanted my uncle to live in the comfort of knowing that I would keep his secret. Keeping the secret in front of us reassured him that I wasn't bothered by it. He knew I could be trusted. There were days I wanted my family to know, particularly my dad. But Mick asked me to remain silent, and so I did. I was silent.

Honestly, the silence didn't feel like a burden but rather a calling, a purpose. Like Miriam, Moses's sister, standing on the edge of the Nile river, I was protecting the special one. I was protecting the one who had a calling on his life. In some ways, I had a sense that my uncle was going to save my family, not through some kind of great act of faith but by helping us fiercely employ our faith as it was challenged and tested. We believed certain truths about the created world—about humans, men and women, sex, and relationships. It was clear to me even at a young age that this subject, my uncle's sexuality, was to be avoided at all costs. So it wasn't difficult to keep silent with my family; it was natural and perhaps even expected.

But with Mick, I wrestled with it. I asked questions: ignorant questions, biblical questions, questions about life and faith. In my head and my heart, I held this piece of my uncle's story that had caused him great fear and shame; but for me, there was something special—dare I say holy—about his suffering: we could talk about it, and he could share his fears with me. This secret was like an open door into a world of vulnerability, as we conversed about love, life, and relationships, but also fear, death, and shame. It was as if the secret gave me access to hidden places in my uncle's heart. Our relationship grew, but so did Mick's understanding of God.

"God loves me," he said one day. "I know that now. I've been going to the church your grandma used to go to."

"You go to church, really?" my brows furrowed.

"Yep, and I am getting baptized!"

"Wow, really? That's incredible!" I probably seemed more surprised than excited.

Water People

I wish I could say that I was there to witness Mick's baptism, but I wasn't. You can't go to college three hours away and expect to be a regular part of your family's everyday life.

But I can imagine it. Here was a man who had thought at one time in his life that God didn't love him and that he could never be accepted by God or the church; a man who for the first time in his life felt connected to people—religious people, church people—in a deep and authentic way.

Christians are water people. Water tells our story. I can imagine my uncle waiting for the waters of baptism to trickle over his head, with the words of God's story spoken over his life: *When nothing existed but chaos, you swept across the dark waters and brought forth light.* Hope. Light. Isn't that what Mick had been looking for? A glimmer of hope in a world that too often felt like darkness and rejection? *In the days of Noah, you saved those on the ark through water. After the flood, you set a rainbow in the clouds. When you saw your people as slaves in Egypt, you led them to freedom through the sea.*

There Mick stood, on the banks of the baptism waters, hoping those waters would bring light, not darkness; peace, not anxiety; life, not death. Isn't that what Moses's mother and sister were hoping for? Although unnamed in their own narrative, in the larger story of God's people, they are Jochebed and Miriam. They stood on the banks of the Nile River—a body of water known for its ability to give life, to make the land fertile. Even the princess of Egypt entered the waters for its life-giving possibilities. But that body of water that was so known for life had become, for an entire people, a graveyard for infant sons. These women stood on the banks of the water, wishing, hoping, and praying for life.

It's a strange kind of story, because who thinks to make a basket out of reeds and place their child in it? On the surface, as a momma, I am horrified by the thought. What if the basket had sunk, gotten torn to pieces by the current, been eaten by the crocodiles, or gotten caught in a fishermen's net? Worry, anxiety, fear—that's what I would have been filled with, and maybe Jochebed is too, but maybe, just maybe, she's fierce.

Think about it: this woman, this slave woman, came up with a detailed plan for saving her son. She used all of her resources. Jochebed was an ancient engineer, crafting a small "ark"—a waterproof, but breathable, vessel for her son. She was a detective, conducting a personality profile on the Egyptian princess, recording her visits to the river's edge. She was a fierce leader, enlisting her daughter's help to execute her strategy, even down to the dialogue that she must have with the Egyptian princess. This was no desperate Hail Mary attempt to save her son. No, Jochebed knew exactly what she was doing. And through Jochebed and Miriam, what Pharaoh intended for death, God purposed for life!

"But when she could hide him no longer, she got a papyrus basket for him and coated it with tar and pitch. Then she placed the child in it and put it among the reeds along the bank of the Nile. His sister stood at a distance to see what would happen to him" (Exodus 2:3-4). Miriam was standing silently at the water's edge, waiting for words of hope, of life, of new possibility. So was Mick. *Pour out your Holy Spirit, to bless this gift of water and Mick to receive it, to wash away his sin and clothe him in righteousness throughout his life, that, dying and being raised with Christ, he may share in his final victory. Mick Fast, I baptize you in the name of the Father, and the Son, and the Holy Spirit, Amen.*

And as Mick experienced his new life in Christ, I, too, waited on the river's edge—in silence like Miriam, listening for the princess of Egypt to call to say "the time has come for you to save your brother." But the time came sooner than I wanted. Although Mick had lived with HIV for many years, defying the statistics of the time, his medical "cocktails" had become more and more complicated.

"Twenty-six pills," he said exasperated. "Twenty-six. That's how many I have to take every day to keep me alive."

Between the pills and their ever-growing side effects, Mick soon questioned the viability of his future. "I need to retire," he declared. And within what seemed like months, he had secured a medical retirement.

But Mick still had dreams. He had always wanted to open his own junk—I mean, antique—shop, and soon was launching into living out his dream of being a store owner.

"We will call it Ruby's," he said.

When my dad and mom asked about his medical condition, because they were going to be part of his support, Mick told them he had a rare blood disease, a form of leukemia.

"It can't be cured, but I could live awhile," Mick told them. By this time in his life, Mick had a master's degree in half-truths and little white lies.

Eager to help his younger brother live out his dream, my dad said yes to the proposal and, for nearly eighteen months, everything was incredible: the store had its grand opening, customers became regulars, and it seemed the business was a wild success. But as the stress of owning a small business wore on my uncle, his health began to deteriorate, and—at least from my perspective—he began to search more and more for a viable exit strategy. When life got desperate and dark, it was easy for my uncle to want to run.

I became increasingly frustrated with my uncle. I was a seminary student and expecting my first child. My husband,

Jon, and I had decided to keep the gender of the child a surprise, but we were delighted at the thought of being parents. We had had trouble getting pregnant. Months turned into a year, and after that year passed, we began talking about seeing a fertility doctor. Not many in their early twenties think that they are going to have so much trouble getting pregnant, but there I was, twenty-three and then twenty-four years old, not able to conceive.

I knew the statistics. I took all the tests. I kept track of my temperature. But with every negative pee-on-a-stick result, I became increasingly depressed. I'd never imagined that getting pregnant would be so hard! At nights, I tossed and turned wondering what was going wrong. What if I never got pregnant? What if I never had kids? I had a plan and this wasn't it. It wasn't until my husband and I stopped trying that we finally became pregnant.

"It was the stress of it all!" my mom said with celebration. She, too, had struggled to conceive at first. She married my dad at the ripe old age of twenty and didn't have my brother until she was twenty-six. This kind of waiting is so painful and so hard. Identities, dreams, and would-be stories, all wrapped up in our body's ability to make a white stick turn blue! But when it did, I couldn't believe it—my own little miracle. I told my Uncle Mick before I even told my parents.

"We're pregnant!" I said over the phone, "But don't tell anyone!" I nearly shrieked with joy when I told him.

Adeline Marie Billups was born October 10, 2005. It was the day before the birthday of my maternal grandmother, Marcella Marie, and two days before the birthday of my paternal grandmother, Ruby Adeline. Mick drove down with my sister to meet us in the hospital and celebrate. He'd known she would be a girl, and he had a red Christmas dress in hand when he arrived at the hospital.

"She's here!" he announced as he threw open his hands, eager to hold this precious little baby. "She's beautiful, Rachel."

And she was! Not the kind of beautiful that people say because they want to be nice to the parents when, in reality, they are looking at some alien life form, but the kind of beautiful you see in an angel child with enough natural hair to be considered a toupee. And Mick, my Mick, was here to celebrate this day.

Sometime later, while looking at her pictures from the hospital, Mom asked, "Does Mick look different to you?"

You see, Mick loved tanning beds. He always wanted to glow. "I'm going to die someday anyway," he would always say. "So why not go out looking good!" But his regular golden brown recently seemed to be a shade of gray. I didn't think much of it, until the phone calls started coming.

"Rachel, I am sick. I am at the hospital."

"Do I need to come?" I asked.

"No, not yet. It's too far from my heart to kill me."

After that call, our conversations became less frequent. But my parents, becoming more and more concerned about his health, would say to me, "Have you talked to Mick lately?"

"Actually, no," I would say.

Then, at one point, my mom replied, "Rachel, I am concerned. He's not been well enough to be at the store."

"Really? I wonder what's going on." I said.

Sometime after that—I don't know if I called or just happened to be in town for a family funeral—Mick and I had a conversation.

"What's up with you?" I said. "Mom and Dad are concerned about you, the store, and your health."

"I just can't handle the side effects anymore! I can't do it anymore, Rachel. Twenty-six pills that make me feel depressed, that rob me of my life. I can't eat, I can't sleep. I am just numb! This is no way to live. I am done," he announced.

"Done? What do you mean 'done'? You can't be 'done'!" I protested. "You are living your dream!" I tried to cheer him up by talking about some of his favorite stuff, and besides I wanted to tell him about the really cute thing that Addie had done that week. But I was so focused on my little girl that I don't think I really heard what my uncle was trying to say. He was done, but I wasn't listening.

By December, Mick had become increasingly sick. There would be no annual Christmas Open House this year. I was disappointed, but I understood. For years my uncle had decorated his home during Christmas like something out of *Country Living* magazine. More than forty Christmas trees adorned his small, antiqued house. Two years prior he had flown Jon and me home for the weekend just so we could see it!

"No matter what it costs. I want you here and I will pay for it." And he did. Well, sort of. "I've got credit," he proclaimed with pride. And on the credit card the tickets went.

Christmas was everything to Mick. His bedroom was decorated in Christmas, so "I can wake up to Christmas morning every day!" He was obsessed. Every square inch of his house; what he wore, what he sang; the cookies, the presents. Mick spared no expense when it came to Christmas. When we came home that year we were eager to celebrate Adeline's first Christmas with family, and we did—with everyone except Mick. He was staying with a close friend, too sick and weak to really join in on the fun. But I couldn't miss a Christmas without at least seeing my uncle, so we decided to visit. We thought that if he saw Addie, it would cheer him up.

But when we arrived, we immediately noticed that he was distant, cold—mentally and physically—and seemed to be everywhere else but in the room with us.

"Can I get another blanket?" he asked. He was already covered in what seemed to be half a dozen.

The life of the party that I once knew as my uncle seemed as docile as a toddler suffering from an ear infection. We talked a little, hugged a little, but that was it. We made a quick exit, and I left mad. Mad because this was Addie's first Christmas, mad because Mick was sick, but honestly, mad because I thought my uncle had given up. He'd stopped taking his pills; he'd stopped fighting the disease. This is what full-blown AIDS looked like, and it was going to take my uncle's life.

The Blow-Up

We had barely made it home when we got the phone call that my great-grandpa, Walter Fast, had died. Grandpa Walter was an incredible man. He was over six feet tall, and he had the kindest eyes that would melt any fear you had of his tall stature. My great-grandpa loved Jesus and the church. It was my great-grandpa who introduced my dad to church, since Dad's own parents, growing up, didn't have much to do with Jesus.

We came home for the funeral but had a limited amount of time to spend. Jon was a lady's varsity basketball coach for the high school, and I would soon be back in class. We'd planned to fly in and out in a couple of days, and on the way out we would stay with my brother. We wouldn't even have time to see Mick at the hospital. I talked with Mick over the phone, but it just wasn't the same. I longed to see him.

By this time, my dad knew. Mick had to tell him. He was too sick, too weak, and too close to death to keep it a secret any longer.

"Rachel," Dad said, "Why didn't you tell me?" My dad was upset because of the time and resources he had invested in my uncle's business.

"I didn't think about it. Mick asked me to keep the secret, so I kept it," I said without hesitation. Didn't I get brownie points for being loyal?

My mom and dad stood somewhere between being afraid of losing Mick and being absolutely livid at his deception. This was an opportunity for shady theology to invade their minds and hearts: they hadn't ever agreed with his lifestyle, and now this! By this time, I had to field several questions about my uncle. Some I didn't have answers for, and others I chose not to answer.

"Does that even matter now?" I protested.

But when you're mad and grieving, sometimes you grasp for any straw that can make sense of the suffering.

Mick missed Grandpa Walter's funeral; he was too sick and weak to leave the hospital. When we left the funeral, we made our way to my brother's apartment to spend the night. The family came up for pizza, mostly because Mom and Dad were desperate to spend any moment with Addie they could. She was the first granddaughter.

Our dinner conversation soon went south as Jason began asking questions about Mick's stay at the hospital. "I don't understand his cancer. He's not in oncology. He's in infectious diseases. What Jennifer heard the doctors saying doesn't make sense with what Mick told us about his disease. Mom, Dad, Rachel, what's going on?"

I said nothing. Jason knew I knew, and it bugged him. The conversation began to build, the questions became heated, and Jason was ready to blow. We in the Fast family are known for our tempers, so I felt sorry for the neighbors that night. We were in the middle of it, all saying things that I am sure we later regretted, until finally, in what seemed like a plea of desperation, Jason exploded.

"Damn it, just tell me!" he demanded. "Does Mick have AIDS?"

Finally, my dad, realizing this wasn't a matter of keeping a secret as much as it was my brother wanting to be in the know out of real-life grief, said through tears, "Yes, Jason, yes. Mick has AIDS."

Our shouts and anger soon turned into tears, and we were grieving together. And we were angry together because we had no control over this vicious disease that would claim Mick's life. AIDS would take Mick.

Things cooled, and early the next morning Jon, Addie, and I were on a plane back to North Carolina.

This Is the End

I got the phone call in the middle of class. It was Dad: "Rachel, if you want to see him while Mick's still alive, you better come home." It was February. Addie and I flew out immediately.

"I'm here," I said to him with tears in my eyes.

"I love you, Rachel," he said. "Always have and always will."

Addie was nearly five months old and pretty good at entertaining herself, so I didn't have any problems with her in the hospital. She was a good baby, and the whole family was there to provide support, including my mother-in-law, Betty.

Mick had been sent to this small-town hospital because it seemed that the previous larger hospital had been struggling to care for him. I couldn't tell if the struggle was because they were ill-equipped or because they were too scared. I feared the latter. But no one was afraid here. At first, we all suited up to visit my uncle—masks, gowns, gloves—but after a couple days, the suits didn't matter anymore. They weren't for our protection anyway; they were for his.

Mick's ability to have conversations would soon vanish. Sometimes he would open his eyes, other times squeeze a hand, and in the scariest moments, he'd lay nearly lifeless on the hospital bed. I wondered in those times whether he was readying himself to take a final breath.

We took turns caring for Mick, talking to nurses, and watching Addie. It was normal for me and one of his closest friends to care for him, swabbing his mouth, helping him take sips of water, watching for bed sores or any other sign of pain or discomfort. But then one night my mom said, "Let me do that."

Over the years, my mom had grown increasingly frustrated with my uncle. Mick hadn't always treated my mother kindly. She felt made fun of by him, hurt by him, and so I wondered why she would volunteer to care for him in such an intimate way.

I watched my mom dip the small sponge into the water and soak his cracked, dry lips with its contents. She rubbed lotion on his hands and arms. She checked his feet. She made sure that the inside of his mouth wasn't dry and that his tongue wasn't parched, and with each care-filled act she prayed for him. She read Scriptures to him. She said, "Mick, I love you, you know." He did know.

I watched a woman who had every right to be angry with my uncle, every right to stand in the corner with folded arms, and perhaps every right to refuse to be there, not only come to him but forgive him. That was the work. Yes, she cared for his wounds and made sure he was comfortable, but in the process, she let go of her own pain and she forgave. Even as I watched her work, I realized I was witnessing one of the most powerful acts of forgiveness I had ever seen. My mom is no Jesus, but I couldn't help thinking about how Jesus washed Peter's feet.

> *He came to Simon Peter, who said to him, "Lord, are you going to wash my feet?" Jesus replied, "You do not realize now what I am doing, but later you will understand." "No," said Peter, "you shall never wash my feet." Jesus answered, "Unless I wash you, you have no part with me."*
>
> *John 13:6-8*

Peter would go on to betray Jesus in a moment when Jesus needed Peter the most. My mom knew what she considered deception and betrayal from someone she loved the most, but she, like Jesus, washed him anyway.

Mick lingered for a while and then, one night, with nearly every member of my family in the room and then some, Betty started singing, "Peace, peace, wonderful peace." Many in the room joined in. We sang and we said our goodbyes, and the nurse came in to change the bed.

"Why don't you all walk out of the room for a moment," the nurse suggested.

So, we all did, and Mick died.

"He's gone," she said as she reopened the door.

While still alive, Mick had looked like a prisoner in a concentration camp. Now that he was dead, it was clear that AIDS had taken its toll and destroyed nearly everything in its wake—everything except fierce.

My sister and I went to J. C. Penney to purchase red suits for his funeral. Red was Mick's color, and it is mine. The funeral was a celebration of a man who lived life full-tilt, who knew he was loved, and—as evidenced by the church packed with people—who loved others well. At the end of the funeral service, with only my family and I standing before the casket, I sobbed. I was losing my favorite, my confidant, my friend. I wailed. This was deep grief for the man that taught me that fierce comes in all forms, even silence.

But silence has a shelf life: for a season, silence can be and should be a form of fierce, but there comes a day when you have to say something—about families, about life, about suffering.

Although Miriam and Jochebed had their moments of silence in Moses's life, the real silent one was God. For four hundred years, God's people were slaves in Egypt: sobbing for the life they had lost, wailing because of the misery and injustice inflicted by their oppressors. These were God's people, God's favorite. Had God not heard the cries of these people? Why was God waiting? Why was God seemingly silent?

No amount of theological gymnastics or moral platitudes can assuage the deep pain I feel in the pit of my stomach when I ask these questions of God and the Bible. The pain doesn't keep me from wrestling. It's merely uncomfortable. But I press in. Why? Because silence is fierce. At times it is looming and mysterious, but I also understand that silence is critical when it comes to participation in relationships. This is true for creation in relationship with the Creator, but also for our relationships to and with one another.

I once had a professor who regularly reminded our class that the quiet ones, the silent ones, were fully participating. I didn't want to believe him. The extrovert in me wanted to rage against everything he was saying. *How can that be? They say nothing. They don't contribute to class discussion. They might as well not even be there! How can silence be participation?* But participation is presence. And silence is a fierce presence.

When words are not possible, presence is one of the most powerful ways that you and I can overcome those things that seek to distract and destroy us. My silence didn't destroy my relationship with Mick or even with my family. No, it became an invitation just to be and to love. Not to have all the answers, not to have it all figured out, not to always have to fit Mick or myself into the right theological categories, but merely to be and to love.

I would love to talk to Miriam. I imagine her as a scared young girl, empowered by her mother to be silent, not with a silence used to hide the family's shame, but with a silence that leads to life. She is standing on the banks of the river, praying that those waters bring life. And they do.

Then Pharaoh's daughter went down to the Nile to bathe, and her attendants were walking along the riverbank. She saw the basket among the reeds and sent her female slave to get it. She opened it and saw the baby. He was crying, and she felt sorry for him. "This is one of the Hebrew babies," she said. Then his sister asked Pharaoh's daughter, "Shall I go and get one of the Hebrew women to nurse the baby for you?" "Yes, go," she answered. So, the girl went and got the baby's mother.
Exodus 2:5-8

So What?

Holding secrets can be a powerful privilege, but when paired with pain can destroy lives. Have you ever been asked to hold someone else's secret? Was this an opportunity for you to hold a life-giving confidence or was this secret a source of shame?

Who taught you to talk about hard subjects? How did this go with your family? Did it create a tension-filled room ready to explode in the moment, or did your family deploy a series of avoidance tactics?

Not all secrets are created equal, and not all secrets are safe for you or others to keep. It is really important to make sure the secret you are holding is not jeopardizing your life, the lives of others, or the lives of people groups. What unhealthy secret do you need to tell?

Presence can be fierce. When has being silent been the most life-giving action you could take for yourself or for others? Silence can be fierce.

❧ 9 ❧

MENTORSHIP

*Don't let anyone look down on you because you are young,
but set an example for the believers in speech, in conduct,
in love, in faith and in purity. Until I come, devote
yourself to the public reading of Scripture, to preaching
and to teaching. Do not neglect your gift, which was given
you through prophecy when the body of elders laid their
hands on you.*

1 Timothy 4:12-14

Fierce Leadership

F ierce leadership is passed from one generation to the next. Learning from and receiving the fierceness of a leader does not depend on an individual's qualifications. Neither a resume nor a string of educational requirements guarantees an extra dose of fierce. Rather, fierce can be imparted through spiritual experience and the Holy Spirit. When we experience fierce leadership, we learn from it and wrestle with it until it shapes us from the inside out.

There's no way young Timothy had any idea what he was getting himself into when he was partnered with Paul. There's biblical evidence that Timothy was young, maybe even as young as fourteen, when he joined Paul on his missionary journey. I'm the mother of a thirteen-year-old, and I can't imagine letting my teenager trek around the Roman world with a tentmaker-turned-street evangelist.

But it seemed that Timothy came from a long line of fierce followers of Jesus. Paul wrote, "I am reminded of your sincere faith, which first lived in your grandmother Lois and in your mother Eunice and, I am persuaded, now lives in you also" (2 Timothy 1:5). Here's a line of women who imparted their fierce love for Jesus to their son and grandson, Timothy. In the Book of Acts, we discover that Timothy's dad was Greek and raised young Timothy as such. Even though his mother was a Jew and later a believer in Jesus, Timothy's father had the spiritual influence over the family. At least Timothy seemed to be raised immersed in Greek culture and religion. We know he never converted to Judaism, since in Acts we learn that young Timothy needed to be circumcised. So I have no idea what led Timothy to follow Paul into the great unknown, other than his deep faith in Jesus and the movement of the Holy Spirit. Paul's faith and leadership must have been contagious for a young man who had all the freedoms of the Greco-Roman culture to trade it in for a painful procedure and life of risk with Paul.

But Paul saw something in young Timothy. Paul saw potential fierce in his faith. And we learn that an entire group of leaders in Lystra laid their hands on young Timothy and spoke prophetic words of life over his future. Words matter! I cannot overemphasize the power of words. A life-giving word creates new pictures of God possibilities in our lives, and a negative word becomes a self-limiting prophecy. Words are the fuel to every "I can" but the darkness of every "I can't." Paul knew the power of words and wrote often to the fledgling disciple. Paul spoke direct and power-filled words to Timothy: "Don't let anyone look down on you because you are young, but set an example for the believers in speech, in conduct, in love, in faith and in purity" (1 Timothy 4:12). In other words, "So what if you are young? Lead away."

Being young isn't all it's cracked up to be. In the fall of 2008, I found myself being selected for the first class of the Young Pastors Network (YPN). The Young Pastors Network was the brainchild of Pastors Adam Hamilton and Mike Slaughter. When they looked across the country, they realized many large church pulpits would be vacated over the next decade. Adam and Mike decided they could offer their gifts and wisdom to a new generation of clergy, some of whom would be filling those pulpits.

I was serving as a resident pastor at Evangelical United Methodist (EUM) Church in Greenville, Ohio. Pastor Bill Lyle had grown EUM Church from a congregation of ninety to more than nine hundred over the course of fourteen years. All of this happened in a town of about thirteen thousand people. And I was sent to learn from this man who had ignited a miracle. The residency program sought to take young clergy and fast-track them into serving as senior pastors in significant churches.

When I applied for the residency program, I had no intention of actually receiving the appointment. Although I have always been an avid learner, I told the interview team that I wasn't interested in serving a large church. I wanted to serve a small congregation in the inner city, where my gifts and theology could be used wisely. The team had other plans.

I found myself in the rural town of Greenville, Ohio, home to the Darke County Fair and Maid-rites. Maid-rites are loose-meat hamburger sandwiches with cheese, onions, and a pickle—basically manna from heaven. Our first gathering for YPN would piggyback on Ginghamsburg's Change the World Conference. I was excited, but there was just one small problem: I was pregnant and due a month before Change the World started.

Ginghamsburg was clear: conferences were not the most comfortable environments for participants with children, no childcare would be provided, and "Please do not bring your infant." Although I am now a little more understanding as to why, Ginghamsburg has a full childcare and preschool center that runs Monday through Friday, with no room for extra kids.

I was frustrated. How can these two men expect to pour into young families if I can't bring my nursing infant? I called Ginghamsburg and was directed to Karen Smith. Karen was the team lead for all Change the World Conferences and talked with me about the limitations of the building. "It's not that you can't bring your baby, Rachel," Karen stated. "We just want you to be focused on the full experience and not focused on taking care of your child. You can bring an infant, but you might find caring for your infant in the middle of sessions distracting."

Visions of Adeline and seminary at Duke Divinity School flashed through my head. I took Addie to class on a number of occasions, but once she started to crawl, it was game over. She was a distraction to me, my classmates, and the professor attempting to teach the class. If only I'd had a quiet child. Nope, no such luck. Karen wasn't wrong; it just was frustrating. She could hear the displeasure in my voice.

"If you want," she offered, "you could wait and be a part of the next class of Young Pastors."

"Wait?" I questioned. "Nope, I am not going to wait. No thanks, I'll figure it out."

Christopher was four weeks old and taking a bottle by the time I arrived at our YPN event. Karen Smith had set up a room for me to pump in, and I was able to fully participate in the week's activities. When I walked into the room of young clergy across the connection, I felt awkward; my four-week postpartum body felt cumbersome to say the least. To make matters worse, my hormones were vacating my body at a rapid speed, and on their way out had left this cheek-sized crater on the side of my face! I didn't feel as if I was looking my best.

"You can do this," I said, giving myself a pep talk before entering the room. It didn't help that some of my classmates from Duke didn't even recognize the postpartum Rachel, and so in my mind, all of my insecurities were validated.

But soon, all that anxiety would leave as I listened to Pastor Mike Slaughter talk about his experience at Ginghamsburg Church. "When I came to Ginghamsburg, there were ninety people in this little old church building," Mike said, "and after the first year I grew it down to sixty." We all laughed. Mike's passion and Spirit-filled confidence were inspiring for a would-be young pastor.

Somehow, Pastor Mike had been able to grow a megachurch in a cornfield without compromising his passion for God's mission to reach the least and the lost. Soon after his talk on church renewal, Mike began speaking on one of his favorite subjects: personal leadership.

"Leaders lead!" Mike declared as if commanding us to action. "You can't lead others where you yourself aren't willing to be led. That's why you've got to take care of the one body God has given you."

"A few months ago, I was in Hawaii with Wayne Cordeiro," Mike began his story. "We were with a bunch of young pastors. We had talked with the group about how all leadership begins with self-leadership. I told them what I told you about my own heart scare at forty-nine years old and how I had to make changes. The very next day, Wayne and I asked all of these twenty-nine-year-olds to go out and run with us. And you know what? At fifty-seven years old, we beat them all."

I don't remember what Mike said next. I just remember thinking, *What? Here I am, a twenty-seven-year-old former college runner, and that old man would have beat me too! That cannot happen! I will never let Mike Slaughter beat me.* In that moment, I was in the worst shape of my life, and it wasn't just the pregnancy: I didn't eat well, I wasn't exercising, and I certainly was not taking time to lead myself.

What Pastor Mike Slaughter didn't know was that his challenging words would send me on a journey to find my fierce—a fierce that was fully embodied. I knew I would never be the leader I could be if I didn't take care of myself, mind, body, and spirit. It was time to put my running shoes back on—well, almost time.

It took me several more months, but soon I was on my way to running my first 5K in six years. After that, I ran a 10K, then my first half marathon, and then a marathon. My number two strength is competition. It doesn't matter what it is; tell me there is a race to win and I am in every time. I had wanted to beat Mike and now I could. He had ignited my road back to health. All this happened because a fierce leader challenged me to find my own embodied fierce. This kind of fierce was hard work, and it didn't happen overnight. It came with the gradual discipline of putting one foot in front of the other and making my health and life a priority.

I was beginning to realize that fierce wasn't a moment; it was a new way of living. Fierce was a lifestyle that would shape all aspects of my life, including my health, my family, my relationships, and even the way I spent my free time. But fierce isn't a lifestyle you can maintain on your own. You need people—pictures of fierce that feed into you. For me, that meant needing folks like Mike and his example in my life. I just didn't realize how quickly I would get what I needed.

Fierce Is Awkward

I can only imagine the kind of mentor Paul must have been to young Timothy. Paul was hard, focused, and a truth-teller. If you were with Paul, you were with Paul. Paul never held back when it came to sharing his wisdom and conviction. Remember that Paul wasn't the encourager; that was Barnabas. At one point, things got so heated between the truth-teller and the encourager over one of their mentees that they had to part ways.

Some time later Paul said to Barnabas, "Let us go back and visit the believers in all the towns where we preached the word of the Lord and see how they are doing." Barnabas wanted to take John, also called Mark, with them, but Paul did not think it wise to take him, because he had deserted them in Pamphylia and had not continued with them in the work. They had such a sharp disagreement that they parted company. Barnabas took Mark and sailed for Cyprus, but Paul chose Silas and left, commended by the believers to the grace of the Lord.
Acts 15:36-40

It's not difficult for me to imagine Paul as having a similar disposition to that of Mike Slaughter. Pastor Mike admits to having the gift of "spiritual irritation." But I will never forget the first time I introduced myself to Mike. It was our second YPN gathering, and this time we were in Florida for a couple's retreat. Adam and Lavon Hamilton and Mike and Carolyn Slaughter had invited members of the YPN and their spouses to an all-inclusive resort. It was awesome! When we arrived, Jon and I pinched ourselves. We had never experienced anything as nice as this.

And it wasn't just the accommodations. These pastors and their spouses spent four days pouring into us. It was powerful. But on the first day, Pastor Mike was doing something that I would later discover was way outside his comfort zone. He was going table to table, engaging in small talk. When he came to our table, he talked to one of our friends and then looked at my husband and said, "What church do you pastor?" My husband quickly reported, "Oh, I am not the pastor, she is."

> Can you look back over your life and point to people who spoke life into you? Certainly, we can point to those self-limiting prophecies, but what about the life-giving ones?

Clearly embarrassed, Mike turned back to me and said, "What seminary did you attend?"

"Duke Divinity School." I said.

"Really, their Christology is excellent, but their praxis sucks!"

I didn't know how to respond. But before I could, Mike was onto his next question, "What church do you serve?" he said.

"Evangelical United Methodist Church," I quickly piped back.

"Oh, I heard they are dying," he retorted, and before I could even say a word, Mike was off to the next victim—I mean, table. It's pretty hard to offend someone three times in your first real conversation, but somehow Mike did.

"Who does he think he is?" I said to my husband. "He's not kidding when he says he is not great at one-on-one conversation. That was painful." And it was, but I didn't let that first conversation bother me too much. Besides, we were spending four days in paradise, and as young parents, we were determined to enjoy every minute of it.

But the very next day at breakfast, Mike was entertaining a table of young clergy with his stories. They were laughing and talking. Just as I walked by, he stopped mid-sentence and said, "Rachel Billups." I couldn't believe he remembered my name. "Rachel Billups, I am your champion."

"Ooo-kaaay," I said. And as I began to walk away, he grabbed my arm.

"No, really, I mean it, I am your champion." And then went back to talking. It seemed a little strange to me that the guy who had, just the day before, offended me three times in one conversation decided that today he was "my champion." But I thought, *Okay, I'll take that over being offended any day.* I had no idea that Mike's words that day would be a prophetic word spoken of promise. He was my champion.

We Need Champions

Do you have champions? Do you have mentors in your life? People who are not afraid to say "I believe in you" and mean it? Can you look back over your life and point to people who spoke life into you? Certainly, we can point to those self-limiting prophecies, but what about the life-giving ones? We need folks who speak life over the next generation, and we need to be those folks: bosses, coaches, friends, parents, and yes, even pastors. I need, you need, the new generation needs people who are willing to say, "I believe in you."

What happened next at YPN could only be described as both life-giving and strange. For the remainder of my time there, Mike seemed to focus in on me. He wanted my opinion about certain topics, wanted to know what I was doing in ministry, and wanted to know how this experience was shaping my life. On more than one occasion, I felt put on the spot, but I also felt favored. I really did sense that Mike was championing my call.

By the end of YPN, I was moving on to my first church, Shiloh United Methodist, as senior leader. I knew I needed a mentor, and I knew I wanted that mentor to be Mike. So, I thought, *What could I do or say to Mike to get him to be my mentor?* Mike Slaughter was a busy man. He didn't have time to pour into all fifty of us on a regular basis. But I mustered up some fierce, walked right up to the man, and said, "Pastor Mike, I want you to put your money where your mouth is! You said that you were my champion. Well, prove it. I am going to be the lead pastor of Shiloh Church and I need you to mentor me." I assumed that he would have to think about it and get back with me. I already had my rebuttal planned. So when he said, "Yes, I will mentor you," it threw me off a little bit.

"Yes?" I questioned.

"Yeah, just get with my assistant, Catherine, and we can meet about four times a year. It's going to be on you to figure out what you need from me."

Mike knew himself well, and he knew the limitations of his time—yet another fierce lesson I would come to learn from him: know who you are as a leader.

"Rachel, we are very similar and yet different," Mike would say. "There are things that you love to do that I could not do."

And we are different. For starters, I am an extrovert who loves to be around people, and Mike Slaughter is not so much. When I invite Mike and Carolyn over to my house, he always wants a count of how many people are going to be there. If there are too many, he just flat-out refuses to show up. A house full of people can be a real drain for Mike. For me, people give me life. I want to win, sure, but more than winning, I want to be on the winning team.

Yet despite our differences, Mike Slaughter was going to be my mentor, and I couldn't believe it. I was delighted knowing that I would be not just mentored but mentored by one of the best—someone who knew how to form a winning team!

Don't Be Afraid to Ask

I had no idea Mike's yes would change my life. When I came up to Ginghamsburg for my mentoring sessions, we would spend hours talking about the challenges I was facing.

"Mike," I said once. "There are two hundred fifty people in my church; one hundred of them are on committees. We have meetings nearly every night of the week! It's killing me, and although we get something accomplished, it seems like it takes weeks to get anything done."

"Rachel, I want you to create a plan and bring it the next time we meet," Mike said.

So, I did. And over the course of the next six months, it felt like the leadership of Shiloh made twenty-five years' worth of changes.

Those mentoring sessions became brainstorming sessions, and it wasn't just Mike and me. If he didn't know an answer to one of my questions, he would pull in a member of Ginghamsburg's lead team to guide our conversation.

For instance, I'll never forget a conversation we had about the importance of excellence in music. He had brought a staff member into his office and asked, "What brought you to Ginghamsburg Church, and why did you stay?"

The staff member replied, "First the music. The music drew us in, but we stayed because of your messages, Mike, and we were inspired by the mission. Here at Ginghamsburg, it's all about the mission."

"The music, the messages, and then the mission?" Mike questioned.

"Most definitely!" the staff member declared.

Mike seemed surprised by the response. I don't think he'd expected music to rank that high on the staff team's list. That one conversation changed the way Mike thought about the excellence of music at Ginghamsburg.

Even though each of our meetings was supposed to end at a certain time, when that time came, Mike would pull me into his next meeting so I could see the inner workings of Ginghamsburg Church. Nothing was off-limits for me. Once Mike invited me and the chair of my leadership board to a board retreat. This was inner-circle stuff, and I had a front-row seat to watching incredible staff members and servant-leaders in action. I couldn't believe the kinds of things they were dreaming about: Christmas Miracle offerings, work in

Sudan, the possibilities of a new church plant, and many others. My experience with Mike was a gift. Mike taught me that fierce leadership had to be shared. He couldn't just hoard all his fierce; he had to give it away. And I was eager to receive it.

I Am Giving My Job Away

Soon Mike was asking me to recruit for an open position at Ginghamsburg. "Rachel, who do you know that could do this job? I want someone just like Rachel Billups." Mike did, but he refused to recruit me. He understood the political dynamics involved in recruiting an up-and-coming leader in the annual conference. I called friends and began recruiting.

"If Ginghamsburg isn't thriving, we all aren't thriving," I said to friends and colleagues across the connection. I said it because I believed it. Months passed, and things didn't work out with the first batch of recruits, so I tried again. But this time, as I was making telephone calls, I had this nagging feeling that I was giving my job away.

I loved Shiloh Church, loved what was happening among the people, and loved being a senior pastor. I had no reason to want to leave. I certainly didn't want to go back to being under someone else's vision. But I couldn't help the nagging feeling in the pit of my stomach.

"Am I giving my job away?" I asked my then spiritual director, Sister Betty. "What should I do? I don't want to leave my church, but I can't stop thinking that this is what I am supposed to do. I am crazy. I make a terrible second-chair leader. I dislike every minute of it."

"Rachel," she said, "do you respect Pastor Mike?"

"Absolutely."

"Do you think he's a person with spiritual wisdom?" she remarked.

"Of course," I replied.

"Then call him and find out what he thinks about it."

Okay, I thought. *It is just a phone call.* I don't think I made it to the parking lot before I said a prayer and dialed Mike's number. I fully expected to leave a voicemail, but he answered. "Rachel Billups, how are you?" he said with a smile in his voice.

"I'm great, Mike," I said, "do you have a minute to talk?"

"Well," he answered, "I'm on a boat at the lake near my cabin. Our entire worship-design team is on retreat. We were all swimming in the lake, but I just happened to get back in the boat when you called. It's just you and me in the boat. Seems like you've got something that we need to talk about. So, what's going on?"

"Well, Mike, you know how you've been asking me to recruit for you. And the last time it didn't work out. You asked me to find someone like Rachel Billups. But you know, Mike, this time, when I make these phone calls, I feel like I am giving my job away. Could it be that I am called to come be part of the Ginghamsburg team?"

I think what I had to say both delighted and shocked Mike Slaughter all at the same time. "Well, Rachel, let's listen for the Spirit's leading. After this worship-design retreat, let's consider what this would mean for you and for Ginghamsburg."

Mike didn't wait until the end of the retreat. I think I received an email that day with an application. It wasn't long before I was interviewing with Ginghamsburg's leadership board and walking through a series of steps that would lead me to what I thought would be my final step to serving at Ginghamsburg: the bishop, my bosses' boss. Ultimately, it was the bishop's call as to whether I would be joining Ginghamsburg.

When I walked into the bishop's office, I had everything ready in my head. Politely, the bishop allowed me to recall all of the events over the last several weeks, and he could see that I was excited about the possibilities. But when I got to the part where I said, "and this is where you get involved," he very politely reminded me that my life is not my own and, at this time, the folks at Shiloh needed me and my leadership. In other words, it was a no. I would not be going to Ginghamsburg. I was more than disappointed; I was devastated.

After leaving, I stopped at a gas station to sob. It took me forty-five minutes to calm down enough to call Mike Slaughter. I couldn't quite wrap my mind around this no, and calling Mike was difficult.

"Mike," I said with a quiver in my voice. "It's a no."

"It's a no," he said. Mike seemed disappointed but also angry. "Rachel, no does not mean never. You keep praying, and I will keep praying about your future at Ginghamsburg."

Dealing with Disappointment

When the door of opportunity is closed in your face, what do you do with it? How do you respond to no? It's a lot easier to deal with the no when you are in control of the decision, but when you are not in control, how do you deal with the disappointment? What amazed me was not my reaction—I was pretty much a mess—but Mike's reaction. With grace and gentleness, Mike affirmed my purpose and my call.

"Rachel, you are an incredible leader and pastor," he said. "So, let's listen to the wisdom of the bishop. We need to see the Holy Spirit's work in this."

I don't like being told no. I am not used to it. But this wasn't the first time I had been told no to a God dream that was bubbling within me.

Mike was right, but I didn't want him to be. I wanted to be justified in my frustration and anger. *Come on, God, this seems like a no-brainer.* But God's message is clear: "'For my thoughts are not your thoughts, neither are your ways my ways,' declares the Lord. 'As the heavens are higher than the earth, so are my ways higher than your ways and my thoughts than your thoughts'" (Isaiah 55:8-9). As a pastor, my life is not my own. I belong to a covenant of clergymen and women, and I have given myself to the process. Yes, this independent, bold, don't-take-no-stuff-from-anyone, fierce preacher has given herself to the process.

But that initial no didn't keep Mike Slaughter from pouring into me and my life. My love for Ginghamsburg and our mentoring relationship gave me an all-access pass to everything Ginghamsburg. I was an outsider given a choice seat at the family table, from the Change the World Conference to time spent with staff. I was able to use the Ginghamsburg family resources to develop my staff, leaders, and volunteers. Ginghamsburg was a gift, even if I was not on the official staff roster. I had no idea of the real-life sacrifices that Mike and his team were making to pour into Shiloh staff and ministry. Some at Shiloh began to jokingly call our church Ginghamsburg South, because Mike's leadership was so influential over my life and the lives of our people.

Your Life Is About to Change

Two years later, in January of 2014, I received the call from my boss: "Rachel, pack your bags. You are going to Ginghamsburg." I was shocked. A couple months earlier, I had sat down with him to tell him my story: the phone call at the lake, the interviews, the bishop's no. He politely listened to my story, although later I learned that he'd already known about the whole thing.

Upon finishing my story, I said to him, "Could it be that I am called to go to Ginghamsburg? If so, send me there. But if not, tell Mike Slaughter to leave me alone."

After getting no response from anyone, not Mike and not my boss, I assumed it was a no for good. So it was a surprise to hear this yes.

Once on staff, Mike continued to be my champion, but things were different now. I was a colleague and no longer a mentee. It seemed to me that Mike's gift of irritation ratcheted up a few notches. Mike noticed changes in me, too.

"Rachel," he said, "Why don't you take notes when I am talking in meetings anymore? You know I'm not always going to be here, and you are going to want to remember some of this stuff."

"Yes, Mike," I said, "I know."

When I joined the team, Mike had planned to transition out of the lead pastor role in 2019. But something happened over the summer of 2015 that made Mike say the time was now. That decision was a real game-changer, for our church, for our staff, and certainly for me. Whereas I thought I had five years of ministry life left with Mike, that now had been cut down to three. I grieved the gradual loss of a daily mentor in my life, the presence of someone I respected so much. I also grieved the loss of a seasoned colleague and friend.

One week prior to Mike's final weekend as Ginghamsburg's lead pastor, he asked me to run a 5K with him. Although both Mike and I knew that this thirty-seven-year-old could now smoke Mike in a 5K any day of the week, he also knew that it would be our last opportunity to cross the finish line together. I told him, "I'd be honored, Mike."

When the gun went off, I knew it would be a race to remember. Mike and I kept a steady pace. Just fast enough to be considered a jog, but not too fast, because we had a lot to talk about: we reminisced about life, ministry, mentoring, and Ginghamsburg Church. Mike told me his dreams for the future and what voice we knew he needed to be for the "big-C" church. This preacher-prophet wasn't finished with ministry; just this season of it.

> Fierce isn't something we can put on a shelf. It cannot be bottled and sold, it is not marketable. But it can be imparted, and that is why I am so passionate about folks sharing their fierce with others.

"I can be even more prophetic if I am not serving the local church," he said. Mike knew the limits of local church life. It's not that church kept Mike from being who he was called to be; it was that Ginghamsburg kept Mike tethered to a people. It's really challenging being both prophet and pastor, and Mike himself will admit that he gravitated to the former.

He shared his concerns for the future and his hopes for Pastor Chris Heckaman, the new lead pastor of Ginghamsburg.

"Rachel," Mike confided, "he's much better with people than I ever could be, and he's exactly what we need." Mike was right. Pastor Chris was incredible with people and had a holy humility that Mike did not have! But it didn't mean that passing the baton of senior leadership to someone new wasn't difficult for Mike.

In that 5K, Mike was real and vulnerable, sharing his deep grief over leaving the people he had loved for thirty-eight faithful years. In that moment, I was Mike's champion and he was mine. It was a solid run, and soon we found ourselves rounding the corner for the final turn. As we were nearing the finish line, he said, "Give me your hand." I thought he wanted to hold hands across the finish line. But I also noticed the finish line was still pretty far away.

"But, Mike," I protested, "we've got a ways to go."

"Rachel, give me your hand," he nearly demanded.

The moment I reached out, he grabbed my hand and began to pray.

"God, like in the days of Elijah, Rachel is my Elisha, and I impart to her a double portion of my anointing. May her ministry, her leadership, and her legacy expand way beyond what mine ever could. In the name of Father, Son, and Holy Spirit, amen." I was shocked, honored, and humbled to know that this man believed so much in me that he would impart his anointing to me.

"Mike," I said through tears, "I am honored."

He looked at me, and with a big smile he said, "Rachel, I am your champion."

Share Your Fierce

I realize that I've been poured into and mentored by so many people in my lifetime: teachers, coaches, leaders, colleagues, and friends. My breed of fierce has been forged by the challenges and cheers of many. But in the last couple of years, I have realized that I am no longer the young one in the group and it's time for me to find a few Timothys to champion and cheer.

Fierce isn't something we can put on a shelf. It cannot be bottled and sold, it is not marketable. But it can be imparted, and that is why I am so passionate about folks sharing their fierce with others. Impartation—the sharing of wisdom, experience, and spiritual gifts—is a highly relational and messy task. Human beings aren't widgets. We don't always receive truth and encouragement very well. Sometimes our hearts and ears are positioned to see and hear what others see. That's why self-leadership is such an important part of finding our fierce. We can't share fierce with others if we aren't aware of our own brokenness and need for vulnerability.

The truth is, I don't need a great-leader highlight reel. I need the pain, the struggle, the Saturday nights when I just want to throw in towel. I need to hear about all the feels— anger, yes; jealousy, yep; but also numbness. I need this when the pain is too much, the problems too big, and the world too broken to feel like I can do a thing about it. Okay, I don't want a mentor who bleeds all over the place, but I don't want one that's totally polished either. I like my mentors just like I like my Bible characters: human, very human.

Perhaps my favorite line that Paul penned to his mentee and colleague Timothy is this, "Greet Priscilla and Aquila and the household of Onesiphorus. Erastus stayed in Corinth, and I left Trophimus sick in Miletus. Do your best to get here before winter. Eubulus greets you, and so do Pudens, Linus, Claudia and all the brothers and sisters" (2 Timothy 4:19-21). Paul's ministry and life were dependent on others. Life was never meant to be lived alone. Paul could not and would not take this fierce journey alone. He had some basic needs—things like a coat for the winter. Winters were rough in a first-century prison. An extended stay there brought with it all kinds of physical and financial needs. Paul needed Timothy. He needed his coworker in the faith. He needed Timothy to be fierce.

Sharing fierce is a two-way street. I find that when I share my experiences of fierce with others, they share theirs with me. In so doing, each of us grows together to become more of who God is calling us to be. Someone shares their fierce with you, then you share your fierce with another, and they another, and then another. That's life, that's faith, and that's real discipleship.

I lead a young adult group in my home. It's kind of a hard pill to swallow when you consider yourself young but then realize that many of the folks in the group were born after you graduated high school. The first time I heard it—"That's the year I was born!"—it was like a sucker punch to the gut. But then I got over myself and realized, *This is exactly how real life works.*

These days, God has given me the opportunity to pour into a young woman named Shelby. Shelby pours her life into the lives of teenagers throughout the Piqua community, but even at her ripe young age, she understands that she, too, needs to be poured into.

"Rachel," she asked me one night, "do you know someone that could mentor me? I am not exactly sure what I am doing with my life. I just know I want to pour my life into other people."

"I guess I am not good enough to be your mentor."

"Oh, no, I would love it if you would mentor me, but I just don't know if you have the time."

"Shelby, I don't, but for you I will make the time." Each week we get together for coffee or lunch and share our broken and beautiful journeys toward finding our fierce.

So What?

Who has shared their fierce with you? Has someone else's fierce ever saved your life?

"All leadership begins with self-leadership." How are you leading yourself? What areas of your life are lacking leadership?

Who is speaking boldly into your life today? Do you have any truth-tellers in your life?

Are you a truth-teller or encourager for someone else? Make a list of the people speaking into you and the people you are speaking into. Name one person you know who needs that encouragement today.

FIERCELY ANOINTED

"Certainly, I will go with you," said Deborah. "But because of the course you are taking, the honor will not be yours, for the LORD will deliver Sisera into the hands of a woman." So Deborah went with Barak to Kedesh.

Judges 4:9

I've always been mesmerized by the story of Deborah. In a book filled with ancient culture steeped in patriarchal practice, the story of Deborah seems like an oasis of personal liberation. Deborah led Israel as a judge for forty years. This woman served as the national and religious leader of God's people. At first, I found myself expecting an explanation in the Bible for this strong female leadership, such as, "Deborah had no husband and therefore functioned more like a spiritual eunuch," or for her story to be paired with an account of the heroic actions of her husband.

But I found no such explanation, no comment or condition. What emerged from the Book of Judges was simply the story of an incredible leader in her own right. This was refreshing! "How did this find its way into the Bible?" I asked right out loud.

God has a way of taking assumptions about God and God's people and turning them upside down. Yet even given this unusual display of wisdom and strength, I am sure Deborah had her fair share of limitations to overcome in order to serve as a leader of Israel.

The pages of the Old Testament drip with cultural expectations for and understandings about women and their place in the surrounding culture: Motherhood? Check. Blind submission to a spouse or male figure? Sure; but, somehow, Deborah defied all of that. Deborah had a fierce identity. She knew her power, her place, and her position. Her calm confidence in that identity is comforting and her brand of self-awareness is contagious. Deborah was true to her role and calling, and she didn't waver in her trust of God and God's anointing. Her leadership was fierce. She was neither celebrated for her motherhood nor venerated for her chaste obedience; rather, she was honored as a prophet with a direct method of communication. Her identity was rooted in fierce and her story inspired the people around her to be fierce as well.

> She sent for Barak son of Abinoam from Kedesh in
> Naphtali and said to him, "The LORD, the God of Israel,
> commands you: 'Go, take with you ten thousand men of
> Naphtali and Zebulun and lead them up to Mount Tabor.
> I will lead Sisera, the commander of Jabin's army, with
> his chariots and his troops to the Kishon River and give
> him into your hands.'"
>
> *Judges 4:6-7*

Deborah's words were clear: "The Lord, the God of Israel, commands you . . . " She was the mouthpiece of God, directing God's people and the Israel army into battle. There's just one catch: for whatever reason, Barak was hesitant. One could assume he affirmed Deborah's leadership and wanted her present for battle. Maybe he experienced her as some kind of spiritual good luck charm or doubted the authority of her declaration. Perhaps Barak wanted Deborah to put her money where her mouth was and come with him to battle. No matter what his reasoning, Deborah interpreted Barak's request as less than courageous and certainly not fierce. Barak did not trust God or God at work in Deborah.

No matter what your previous understanding of women in positions of religious authority, it's got to be challenging to read a story like Deborah's and maintain that God doesn't want women to lead God's movement. If God overcame major cultural expectations to place Deborah in a position of power, why can't we fathom God's desire to do more of the same today? Frequently I find myself in religious circles where men and women are struggling with the question of women in religious leadership. Often, someone speaks up to admit that some of our best women are going to work for the marketplace because the church has underemployed them or undermined their leadership. Deborah was certainly not underemployed and she wasn't relegated to only leading other women. Deborah was face to face with the commander of Israel's army and she was attempting to help Barak claim his fierce, God-given identity as leader.

As a prophet, Deborah was anointed by the power of the Holy Spirit to speak on behalf of God. Her anointing alone would qualify Deborah as a fierce leader, but fierce is more than one moment. Fierce is a lifetime of courageous moments. Finding your fierce means letting go of what you think you need and holding onto the truth right in front of you. Deborah knew the truth—God was with her. God was with her people. God would be with Barak. Barak could win the battle, but his hesitation was steeped in an interesting form of fear-based codependency that kept him from being the leader that God has destined him to be. And his hesitation came with a price.

One can almost sense the tension between Barak and Deborah when Deborah broke the silence: " 'Certainly I will go with you,' said Deborah. 'But because of the course you are taking, the honor will not be yours, for the LORD will deliver Sisera into the hands of a woman.' So Deborah went with Barak to Kedesh" (Judges 4:9). One would assume that the victory would be Deborah's, but it isn't. At the very least, she is not the person who delivers Sisera into the hands of his enemies. Yet Deborah did not allow this or any other form of self-doubt to limit her momentum or the future of God's people. Firmly centered in her authority from God, Deborah helped Barak lead Israel into battle.

Who Am I?

Sometimes we get tricked into thinking that portions of our past or our entire life's narrative prevent us from becoming fierce. For years I wanted to blot out all the rough patches in my life and create one smooth trail. I dreamed of having a different start, a better road to run, or even a more significant shift in my life's work. Dreaming of new possibilities is great, as long as we don't sugarcoat the past. Our failures and mistakes are important to who we are today. They are valuable parts of our stories and who we know ourselves to be. Sometimes in my youth, for example, I wrestled so intently with the question *Who am I?* that it nearly left me paralyzed.

One of these times, at the age of twenty-three, I found myself standing across from a man who had one of the largest congregations in the state of Michigan, serving out his ministry career in the Greater Detroit area. He was Dr. Bill Ritter, and Dr. Bill Ritter knew who he was. He, like Deborah, had an identity firmly planted in the call of God on his life.

A pastor's office sometimes feels like a museum to all things holy. Communion cups, Bibles, and religious artifacts line the shelves and walls, and even sometimes find themselves situated on large desks. Dr. Ritter had one of those desks because he had one of those lives. He seemed to me like an institution. Not the stuffy or outdated kind of institution, but the kind that declared, "I am legend."

But my twenty-three-year old self couldn't grasp that kind of firm identity—or at least not yet. I was a teaching congregation intern at First United Methodist Church in Birmingham, Michigan, and this farm-girl-turned-seminarian felt like a total fish out of water. For starters, I had just spent the academic year interning for Urban Ministries of Durham, a homeless shelter and soup kitchen just miles from Duke University's campus. In contrast, Birmingham was located in one of the wealthiest zip codes in the country. In a matter of months, I went from living in the boonies to living in the city to living in the wealthy suburbs. Perhaps the geographic whiplash had me off-balance; regardless, I was struggling to reconcile how all of this fit into the reign of God.

"Dr. Ritter," I said. "I have to be honest. I've been working with folks who struggle with housing and now I am working with folks who have multiple houses across the country. When I found out I was coming to Birmingham, I began to pray, 'God, help me to understand how people can be rich *and* be

Christian.'" (Sometimes I look back on the kind of unfiltered statements I made to people much wiser than myself, and I am grateful for their grace in the moment!)

"Well, Rachel," Dr. Ritter said, "I believe God will reveal it to you."

These identity conversations became a weekly part of my internship with First Church and my relationship with Dr. Ritter. In one such conversation, I asked, "Dr. Ritter, how did you get here?" I thought there must have been some clues along the way as to why this pastor was so successful, his ministry so contagious, and his identity as a fierce leader so firmly established.

"We both come from somewhat narrow slices of experience and expectation,"[1] Dr. Ritter said. Dr. Ritter was not belittling or even making fun of our places of origin, just naming the limited-future pictures that surrounded us. I'd grown up on the edges of Appalachia and he in the city of Detroit. In other conversations, he also helped me understand that it was his history that fueled the present moments of his life; that "thin slice" helped him to understand and value the whole of people's life experiences. Thin slices gave him perspective and a fire to want more.

What I didn't realize is that our conversations didn't just get me thinking about my identity and past, they also got Dr. Ritter thinking about his. Namely, he began to think about how he would use my question "How did you get here?" to fuel his fierce—and mine.

It was a regular Sunday morning, and I was going to attend a different church as part of an internship I had created within my internship. First United Methodist, Birmingham, was a great place to learn, but I missed being where "real" people were, so I had started traveling to Cass Community Social

Services each week. Director and pastor Rev. Faith Fowler had given me the green light to come and learn from the numerous social services and community partnerships Cass had already established. I was determined to attend worship that morning, not at FUMC, but at Cass Community United Methodist. But when Dr. Ritter heard my plans he said, "Rachel, can you adjust for the morning? I would like you to serve as liturgist and hear my message."

I wasn't exactly appropriately dressed for high-church traditional worship. I needed to borrow a robe, and I had but one option. The only female pastor on staff was barely five feet tall. As I placed my arms into the robe, I knew I was going to look ridiculous. Once on, the robe barely reached past my knees and elbows, but at least my clothes were covered. At the start of the service, I read the Scripture and said the prayers.

Then Dr. Ritter began preaching, and his sermon started with my question:

> When a leader clearly understands his or her God-given identity, it is second nature for that person to pour courage into their surrounding leaders.

"So how did you get here?" I wasn't sure what she meant by "here." Did she mean ministry in general? Or did she mean Birmingham in particular? She was talking about both. Sort of. But, more to the point, she was talking about how one finds one's way—or how one finds God's way—from the place where one begins to the place where one ends.

You see, Rachel and I share something in common. We both come from somewhat narrow slices of experience and expectation. She from the country. Me from the city. And while, in neither of our cases was there all that much holding us back, neither was there all that much pushing us on.

"So how did you get here?" she wanted to know. Meaning all of it. She wanted to know about the strange range of churches I have served, places I have lived, people I have met and experiences I have had, given that there was little in my background that suggested (even hinted) that half of this was possible. When my mother married my father, she moved six miles from her childhood to make her bed with him. And when my father married my mother, he moved four blocks from his childhood to make his bed with her. Which, thirty years later, was the house in which he died. His death occurred following the Detroit riot, one week before he and my mother were scheduled to move. Concerning that move, I think that because his heart wasn't in it, it was no longer up to it. My people were not traveling people. Neither were my people college people. My father, who may have been the smartest man I ever knew, decided to abort the last half of his senior year in high school by hopping a freight train with Louie Malchie. And although he probably explained it as "seeing the world," I think that what he was doing was running from the world. Which may explain why, years later, he chose to stay home rather than attend my graduation from Yale. It had less to do with what I'd just finished than with what he'd never started. I often tell people that when I went to Albion to begin my collegiate journey, I first laid eyes upon it the day I moved into it. I applied because my minister said I should. I never asked why. He never said why. And even though we lived a mere ninety miles from the place I was to spend the next four years of my life, no one in my family ever suggested that we get in the car and check it out. Nor did I think to get in the car and check it out. Although we had a car . . . and enough money to gas it. Do you see what I mean about coming from a narrow slice of experience and expectation?[2]

Dr. Ritter went on to talk about four people who had opened the door—perhaps one could even call it a window—of possibility and expectation for him: Albert Keenan, a high school literature teacher, who saw something in William Ritter that William hadn't even discovered yet; the school principal, Joseph Pinnock, who had the courage to speak the truth in love and challenge Dr. Ritter to strive for academic excellence; a new college professor at Albion College, William Gillham, who challenged Dr. Ritter to think beyond the local seminary options and started the conversation that led him to Yale; and Herb Hausser, Dr. Ritter's first district superintendent, who refused to allow Dr. Ritter to get lazy or develop bad habits in ministry.

Dr. Ritter said each one opened a door or, at the very least, God used them to open doors for him. But then, in typical Dr. Ritter fashion, he closed with this remark: "And that, my dear, multiply talented, amazingly gifted Rachel, is as close as I can come to telling you how I got here."[3]

And that was how he closed the sermon. I was moved and inspired, and I had begun reflecting on the many people who had opened doors of expectation and possibility for me. But that wasn't the end of the message this particular Sunday.

Dr. Ritter asked me to come to the center of the chancel area and said, "Rachel, today I want to open the door for you. You imagine yourself going back to rural Ohio someday and pastoring a church much like the one that you grew up in, but young woman, that's not what I see. Someday you will be leading a large church and your ministry will far exceed anything you've ever dreamed of; let me show you the door."

With that one declaration, Dr. Ritter showed me a level of fierce identity I had never known before. And he didn't just do it once. He declared those words over me after each sermon in all three worship gatherings that morning. Although he probably knew it, on that day, Dr. Ritter changed my life! He painted for me a picture of a fierce identity I hadn't even dreamed about. He became one who showed me the door. He became a Deborah.

> When they told Sisera that Barak son of Abinoam had gone up to Mount Tabor, Sisera summoned from Harosheth Haggoyim to the Kishon River all his men and his nine hundred chariots fitted with iron. Then Deborah said to Barak, "Go! This is the day the LORD has given Sisera into your hands. Has not the LORD gone ahead of you?" So Barak went down Mount Tabor, with ten thousand men following him. At Barak's advance, the LORD routed Sisera and all his chariots and army by the sword, and Sisera got down from his chariot and fled on foot.
>
> *Judges 4:12-15*

Deborah did not back down. Sisera was ready to fight and Deborah commanded that Barak go into battle. "This is your identity, Barak! You are the leader of Israel's army, now go and defend God and God's people." Deborah spoke courage into Barak and his army, and they fought with such fierce that Sisera was forced to flee.

When a leader clearly understands his or her God-given identity, it is second nature for that person to pour courage into their surrounding leaders. It's what Dr. Ritter did for me. He helped me understand that fierce is forged in identity. And that finding our fierce isn't a shedding of our past, a rejection of all things hard, or an elimination of our greatest fears. Finding our fierce is a way of life that is firmly grounded in identity. When you know who you are, where you've come from, and where you've been, you get a clue as to where you are going. And rough patches along the way become the fuel that propels you forward and helps you recognize that everything belongs. It's not a license to keep stepping into the muck of life but rather a perspective on the muck.

> We all need Deborahs—people to remind us that our worth and value do not come from our ability to produce in the moment. We are more valuable than the gifts and wares that we sometimes seem to be peddling.

Rough Patches

I was finding myself in a lot of rough patches. I had been serving as pastor and leader for years, but for whatever reason, I was questioning my call. My transition to Ginghamsburg

Church has been a tough one for me. I had loved my job as the lead pastor of Shiloh United Methodist Church, and I knew I was not transitioning from a bad situation to a good situation. I was moving from a great church to a great church.

But stepping into Ginghamsburg was like stepping into a leadership crucible—pressure, pressure, pressure. Much of the pressure was self-imposed, but some was just the reality of the organization. The expectations were high. Perhaps the greatest challenge I faced was figuring out how to effectively communicate to a megachurch crowd. Although I thought of myself as a solid communicator, this level of expectation exposed all of my weaknesses. During that preaching transition, I remember talking to a colleague and saying, "I feel like Tiger Woods and I'm changing my golf swing. In the long run, I know it will make me better, but right now it just feels awful." And it did. Instead of being energized by preaching, preaching became a place of pain and anxiety, and this quickly had me questioning my call and identity. "I am not sure I can do this," became my mental mantra nearly each time I stepped onto the platform.

One Saturday afternoon, in preparation for the weekend's preaching, I realized I was at the breaking point. Fear-based anxiety had me nearly crippled. I couldn't focus. I was unsettled, and a low panic began to set in. I am not an anxious person, so this form of professional anxiety was totally foreign to me.

"I can't do this," I said to myself.

Was I talking about preaching the weekend? Sure, but more than that, I had determined that I had made a huge mistake leaving my post as lead pastor and attempting to navigate the megachurch world. I'm sure that in that moment my husband attempted to cheer me up or cheer me on, but I wasn't having any of it. The anxiety kept pouring over me and increased with each passing minute on the clock. I knew it was impossible for me to call it quits just hours before the weekend, but I wanted some assurance from others around me.

I called a couple of mentors in my life, colleagues in ministry who know me well and had championed my leadership throughout the years. Voicemail. Voicemail. Voicemail. Not one person picked up the call. I did my best to ready myself for the weekend. I would have to muster my way through five worship celebrations. By the time I left the house, I was in tears, and as soon as my car pulled into the parking lot, I was having a full-blown anxiety attack: the pain in my chest kept me from stepping out of the car. I didn't know what I would do.

"I can't do this! I've got to get out of here!" I said out loud to no one in particular. That's when the phone rang. A familiar voice was on the other line. There was no pretending in this moment, no small talk, and no time to curb my emotion. I was in full panic.

My friend and I didn't talk long. I couldn't talk and certainly didn't have much time before I needed to get myself from the parking lot into the church building. But in a matter of minutes, the friend on the phone had affirmed my anxiety and helped me navigate the moment.

"Rachel, you can do this," she said. "I know you can. I know you, and I know who God's called you to be."

Our conversation was no spiritual pep talk. She also talked with me about whether or not this kind of pressure was healthy for me or our organization. And she said she was more concerned about my identity and call as a beloved daughter of God than my ability to preach a great weekend.

The honesty, vulnerability, and calm nature of this firm friend kept me from being completely debilitated. Her "I know you can" was just enough to dry up the ugly cry and snot long enough to let me get out of the car and into the building. Don't get me wrong. I am one hundred percent convinced that I preached a weekend of mediocre sermons at best. But nevertheless, I preached. Sometimes in our lives, we need people to remind us of who we are so that we can fully step into our fierce. This colleague didn't tell me what to do, give me an easy out, or even question my sanity when I was ready to bail. She listened, reflected, and reminded me of who I am and whose I am.

We all need Deborahs—people to remind us that our worth and value do not come from our ability to produce in the moment. We are more valuable than the gifts and wares that we sometimes seem to be peddling.

"I am only as good as my last sermon," I've heard a colleague declare on more than one occasion. Although it may feel that way, it is just not true. In our consumer-driven culture, we've got to recognize that we are—you are, and I am—a beloved son or daughter of the living God. Our identity pours out of God's presence in our hearts, heads, and bodies. When we firmly understand who we are, we are unstoppable, because no amount of anxiety, no amount of fear, and no amount of folks telling us "you can't" can keep us from God's fierce call of "Oh yes you can—and you will!"

The Anti-Deborahs

Let's talk. There are people in your life who will intentionally and sometimes unintentionally keep you from embracing your fierce identity. People who use their words and lives to block the fierce future that God has for you. Sometimes it's a limitation prophecy spoken over you or a negative comment on social media, but sometimes it is what another person *does* that makes you mad.

You should have seen my face. I couldn't imagine what kind of grown man would come up to a leader and pull her ponytail in front of a group of people! Although I can imagine this gentleman thought he was being playful, I wanted to say to him, "What the hell do you think you are doing? I am not five years old! Don't touch me or my hair!" I am sure my body language communicated most of that to him and to those surrounding me, but I decided to say nothing. In the moment, I decided to let it go and to back down from the situation.

Newsflash: men and women should be asking one another permission to touch each other's bodies. Certainly, grown men have zero permission to touch my hair. Was I fierce in the moment? Maybe—or maybe I wasn't. Sometimes it's difficult to know when to assert your fierce identity and when not to. That's what's so interesting about fierce. Knowing when to remind others of your identity and when to allow them the space to challenge yours. Don't get me wrong, our bodies are our bodies and certainly no one has permission to violate our personal space. But when do we remind people that we are fierce?

I am sure I am not alone. Crude jokes, lingering hugs, and sexual comments are just some of the identity-crushers that men and women face in and outside the church. Just recently, my family and I were at a pool party. A more seasoned gentleman (if I could call him that) asked if I was getting into the pool.

I said, "No, I didn't bring my suit."

Without thinking for a moment, he quipped back, "You don't need one. Just get in the pool naked." It didn't take him long to feel the tension in the air and my husband standing within earshot. "Oh, that's your wife, isn't it?"

"Yes," Jon replied, "She is my wife and she is a pastor."

My husband wanted him to feel not only the discomfort of his comment but also a little embarrassment. The man didn't have words, and neither did I. True confession: sometimes I get tired of asserting my fierce identity.

But tired isn't an excuse. We are interconnected. Men and women are created to be in healthy, life-giving, fierce relationships with one another. It isn't always easy, and we are terribly human, but we must inspire one another to say the hard things, to overcome cultural and social norms, and to be willing to break the silence when people's identities are being violated. The task is beyond standing up for ourselves; we are standing in solidarity with one another, championing a body of Christ, a culture, and a community where men and women are partnered to "fight the good fight." If God could transcend years of cultural assumptions about the role and place of women by partnering Barak with Deborah, then we too can partner to champion the fierce in our brothers and sisters alike. I am the product of both women and men sharing their fierce identity so that I can find my own.

Yet in our humanness, we sometimes believe in a scarcity of anointing. When someone else succeeds, when another person rises to the occasion, when a friend or colleague is honored, we believe that, somehow, this means there is now less fierce to go around. Don't believe that for a second! Our God is a God of abundance, and although we all have a function *in* the body of Christ and the reign of God, every single person can and does have a fierce identity.

It creeps up when you are scrolling through social media. You might read about so-and-so's new book, speaking gig, nonprofit business, record deal, podcast, or fill in the blank, and a low anxiety rumbles within you. Or maybe you think that you are behind others in your personal progress or that you haven't got something they have.

But the reality is that you are gifted and fiercely anointed to be *you*. You be you! Don't freak out or even begin speaking words of limitation over a brother or sister who is kicking tail and taking names. Instead, celebrate, rejoice, and throw a party because, pretty soon, when you understand who you are, when you find your fierce, we are going to be scrolling through your social media, reading your book and listening to your podcast and saying, "Yes! This is the exact brand of fierce this universe needs!"

You Need a Tape

I dusted off the cassette-tape player. (Okay, I know some of you don't know what that is, but hang with me.) I hadn't listened to a tape for a really long time, but I was starting as lead pastor of a church, and so I needed the reminder. Some people just have a voice that, when you hear it, you know that God is speaking. Dr. Ritter has that kind of voice. Before I left as his intern, I asked for a copy of the sermon that he had preached about my question. Somehow, I knew I would need to listen to that sermon again more than one time in my life. I would need to be reminded of my fierce identity. I sat in the garage as I was unpacking boxes and listened to those words again and again and again. I was stepping into the lead role really for the first time in my life. The leader before me was their youngest senior leader and came at forty-seven. And never had the senior leader been a woman. So at the ripe young age of twenty-nine, I stepped into a pulpit I knew my shoes were not big enough to fill and yet Dr. Ritter's words challenged the "I can't" that bubbled within me.

If you think for a second that after you read this book, you are going have a full dose of fierce that never leaks out or needs refilled, think again! Life is too hard and harsh for one moment of courage to propel us forward. Recognize that you will need a whole series of tapes or podcasts or letters or conversations or whatever it is to help you know that you, like Barak, are called to lead. You will need encouragement from the Deborahs in your life to remind you that you are bold, courageous, talented, insightful, gifted, and fierce. You will need to play that tape over and over and over again. Because even though people may attempt to tell you otherwise, you are beloved, you are chosen, and you are fierce!

So What?

Who in your life has lived out his or her fierce?

Can you name a Deborah in your life? What about that person's identity was so contagious?

How did he or she overcome life's obstacles?

What limitations do you imagine as a result your story? What limitations do you place on yourself? Have you ever had moments of "I can't do this"? How did you overcome those moments? How are you overcoming those moments now?

Ever been silent when you needed to be fierce? When were you able to lean on the fierce of others?

ACKNOWLEDGMENTS

I want to express my deep gratitude to Maria Mayo, Susan Salley, and the entire team at Abingdon Press. Your passion and excitement for this project fueled my resolve to share this message with the world. Maria, I cannot thank you enough for the long phone calls, continual encouragement, and the belief that my life experience was worth sharing. I am grateful for your voice in my life!

I am also grateful to Pastor Chris Heckaman, the staff, and the entire movement that is Ginghamsburg Church for giving me the time and opportunity to write, dream, and use my voice to encourage a new generation of Jesus-followers. To Chris, Catherine, Karen, Nathan, Rusty, and Jon: faith is a team sport, and I love that we are a team!

To every single person who poured into my life, attempting to keep the limitation prophecies at bay—Gladys Schaal (my first-grade teacher), Mrs. Hilbert (who inspired me to love writing), Kathy Morris, Nancy Maxson, Larry Maddox, Paul Risler, Joel Hardbarger, Dr. Ritter, Bill Lyle, Mike Slaughter, Wade Giffin, Tim Schoonover, Julie Wilburn-Peeler, Sara Thomas, Marie Smith, Jenn Lucas—you all have spent years speaking life into me!

Now to the folks who did the tedious work of combing through my rough draft: first, I am in a debt of thanks to my mother-in-law, Betty Billups. She pored over every single page, discovered surprises about her daughter-in-law along the way, and in the end, helped me create a more polished product—thank you! And to Kim Miller, my wordsmith. You know me and my words sometimes better than I know myself. You've made me a better writer and a more faithful follower of Jesus. I am so grateful for your friendship and your gifts!

I am honored to be partnered with Jon Billups, my husband, cheerleader, and friend. Your belief in me and God's work through me inspires me to be more. You are magic in my life. To my kids, Adeline, Christopher, David, and Sarah—you inspire Mommy to live a more faithful life!

Finally, to my parents Rick and Linda Fast. Who knew that the seed of faith you planted into that young girl with a fiery temper would blossom into a garden of love for all? You did! I am so grateful for who you are, who you've been, and who you have continued to become because of your love for God and others—thank you, thank you, thank you!

I didn't realize how writing this book would change me. It has given me the space to see just how God has been and continues to be present in my life. I can't believe I have the honor and privilege of sharing my story, and I pray that it inspires you to share your story too!

NOTES

3. Confessions of a Mean Girl

1. National Eating Disorders Association, "Eating Disorders in Men and Boys," www.nationaleatingdisorders.org/learn/general-information/research-on-males.

2. Mary Beth Quirk, "Abercrombie's 'We Only Like Cool Kids' CEO Stepping Down from Throne Made of Cargo Pants," *Consumerist,* December 9, 2014, https://consumerist.com/2014/12/09/abercrombies-we-only-like-cool-kids-ceo-stepping-down-from-throne-made-of-cargo-pants/.

4. Fierce Rebellion

1. "Florida Student Emma Gonzalez to Lawmakers and Gun Advocates: 'We Call BS,'" *CNN*, February 17, 2018, www.cnn.com/2018/02/17/us/florida-student-emma-gonzalez-speech/index.html.

2. Stanley Hauerwas, *The Hauerwas Reader*, eds. John Berkman and Michael Cartwright (Durham and London: Duke University Press, 2001), 257–58.

6. Defining Moments

1. Marianne Williamson, *A Return to Love: Reflections on the Principles of "A Course in Miracles"* (New York: HarperCollins, 1992), 190.

7. Facing the Pharaoh

1. Bishop T. D. Jakes, "Combustible Passion," 2010 Willow Creek Association Leadership Summit. For a summary of the full remarks, see http://henrywill4.blogspot.com/2010/08/leadership -summit-2010-final-session.html.

10. Fiercely Anointed

1. William Ritter, "Four Who Showed Me the Door," *Ritter Writes*, July 25, 2004, www.ritterwrites.com/writings/2017/8/21 /four-who-showed-me-the-door.

2. Ritter, "Four Who Showed Me the Door."

3. Ritter, "Four Who Showed Me the Door."